Dream Life
teen journal

A **30**-Day Guide to
ESCAPING THE DRAMA
~ *and* ~
CHASING YOUR BEST LIFE

DENISE WALSH

DREAM LIFE TEEN JOURNAL by Denise Walsh
1006 Cherry Street SE
Grand Rapids, MI 49506
DeniseWalsh.com
hello@denisewalsh.com

Unless otherwise noted, Scripture quotations are taken from the Holy Bible, New International Version®, NIV®. Copyright © 1973, 1978, 1984, 2011 by Biblica, Inc.® Used by permission of Zondervan. All rights reserved worldwide. www.zondervan.com. The "NIV" and "New International Version" are trademarks registered in the United States Patent and Trademark Office by Biblica, Inc.®

Scripture quotations marked ESV are from the Holy Bible, English Standard Version. Copyright © 2001 by Crossway Bibles, a division of Good News Publishers. Used by permission.

Visit the author's website at DeniseWalsh.com.

International Standard Book Number: 978-0-578-67649-4

First edition

20 21 22 23 24 — 987654321
Printed in the United States of America

Contents

Introduction

Your dreams matter. They do not need to be put on hold until you reach a certain age. Regardless of how crazy your life, schedule, and relationships seem, you can start working toward everything you hope for. That's because unlike a wish, your dream life is the guaranteed result of a journey that combines the right plans, actions, and attitude. That journey begins right now.

Dream Life Teen Journal contains a series of not-so obvious exercises that will help you carry yourself with confidence, build healthy relationships, say goodbye to the toxic ones, and move closer to creating the life that accomplishes all your goals. If you will spend twenty to thirty minutes with this journal each day, you'll learn how to create the space you need to first set your mind and heart and then make an action plan to ensure that each day is productive.

Your Dream Life Goal

Let's be real. Dreaming is a blast, but setting goals can be nerve-racking. The very thought of making a commitment can stir up all sorts of limiting beliefs about yourself, your role in the world, and what you are able to accomplish. Do not be intimidated. I'm going to show you exactly how to choose the first goal that will move you closer to living the life you hope for.

Use the following exercises to choose a starting point.

1. Which of the seven areas of life (i.e., family, friend-ships, finances, health, hobbies, school, and giving back) would you like to work on first?

   _____

2. Why is this area the best starting place for you? Having a clear picture of what makes it important for you to address right now is like gasoline on fire; it will ignite and sustain your commitment and passion for seeing your dreams become reality. I also want you to ask yourself, Is this something I want to focus on, or did I choose it because I think it's what someone else wants for me? Keep in mind, it is healthy to be mindful of your obligations and responsibilities, but it is also important to set a goal you genuinely care about. Through practice, you will learn how to balance the expectations that are placed on your shoulders with self-care practices that will help keep you sane. For now, though, try to select something that will nurture your own physical, mental, spiritual, or relational health.

   _____

   _____

   _____

   _____

   _____

   _____

3. Goals are not set in a vacuum, and no goal stands alone. Every change you make will have a positive or negative effect on another part of your life. With this in mind, how will improvements in the area you

picked in question 1 positively impact other areas of your life?

_____

_____

_____

_____

4. Now's the time to turn your dreams for this area into tangible, realistic, and exciting goals. Start by writing your desires in the left column of the following table. (For now, focus just on your dreams in the one area you plan to start with.) Then on the right, write a goal for reaching that dream.

Try to choose goals that are SMARTER:

- **S**pecific
- **M**easurable and motivating
- **A**chievable
- **R**ealistic
- **T**ime-bound
- **E**valuated
- **R**ewarding[1]

For example, if I decide I want to get better grades, I might set this target goal: "I will maintain a 3.2 GPA or higher in the next three months by earning at least a B in each class." The stated goal is:

- *Specific*. It establishes a clear outcome (a specific GPA).
- *Measurable*. The goal states a specific GPA that will be maintained. It is also *motivating* because the results are clear.
- *Achievable*. If you're unsure what grades you would need to achieve in order to earn the GPA you're reaching for, it's a good

1 Adapted from "SMART Goals: How to Make Your Goals Achievable," Emerald Works, accessed March 8, 2020, https://www.mindtools.com/pages/article/smart-goals.htm.

idea to talk to your teachers and/or guidance counselor. They can help you set achievable goals.

- *Realistic.* Not only should your goal *be* possible, but you must *believe* it is possible.

- *Time-bound.* The goal has a clear end point, three months from now.

- *Evaluated.* As you work toward your goal, you will continually assess the goal and your progress. Your assignment and test grades are a good barometer of your grade, and your teachers should be able to provide an accurate estimate of your standing in their classes.

- *Rewarding.* Along the way, you will celebrate your hard work, tweak your approach and attitude in order to maintain focus and ensure progress, and reward yourself for a job well done.

Be sure to write in the present tense, and be positive. You're welcome to use the following examples as templates.

My dream is:	A SMARTER goal is:
more spending money	I will get a job and work throughout summer vacation so that I can save $1,000 by August.
to be a better athlete	I will be a starter during the next soccer season.
to get along better with my family	For the next three months, I will say yes to improving communication with my family.

5. Goal fulfillment in the area of your life that most impacts the others can initiate a quantum leap forward, so start there. Pick the dream and goal from above that you want to work on first. We will call this your Dream Life Goal, because it will have a cascading effect that will change everything. It will launch you into brand-new territory.

Rewrite it below, and underneath it write how you're going to make it happen. (These are your process, or daily practice, goals.)

Example 1:

My Dream Life Goal is: For the next three months, I will say yes to improving communication with my family.

My daily practice goals are: I will put my phone away and eliminate other distractions so that I can engage with my family when we are together. I will share how I am feeling honestly and respectfully in a way that leads to open communication rather than confrontation. I will do at least one fun thing with my family per week.

Example 2:

My Dream Life Goal is: I will be a starter during the next soccer season.

My daily practice goals are: For the next three months, I will run three miles after school five days a week. I will find a nutrition plan that supports my health goals. I will maintain the GPA needed to play on the team.

My Dream Life Goal is:

_____

_____

_____

My daily practice goals are:

_____

_____

Now pick one or two of these daily practice goals to work on right now. Once you master these and turn these practices into habits, you can move on to the other daily goals that support your big Dream Life Goal.

How It Works

Over the course of this thirty-day journey, there will be lots of repetition. You will rewrite your goal daily. You will rewrite and repeat life-changing affirmations daily. You will take time each day to be thankful for the life you have and to picture in vivid detail the life you dream of. This is intentional. It takes twenty-one days to form a habit, and the goal here is to establish new habits and turn those practices into a lifestyle that will breed success. Resist the urge to skip these exercises because they are the same as what you did the day before. Trust me; taking the time to choose joy now and to cement your dream by visualizing it vividly on a daily basis will bring you closer and closer to achieving it. You are creating new thought patterns and strengthening your identity, so consistency is key.

Before these success habits become normal to you, you may find that they feel tricky or difficult to complete. To help you get comfortable with this routine and create a personal vision of yourself that keeps you excited about your future, I have put together some resources that go along with each day's activities. At the end of this book, you'll find a long list of sample affirmations and fillable templates you can cut out, write on, and post around your room, in your locker, or in your car to help you shift your mindset toward the life of your dreams. You'll also find a set of habit trackers, which will make it easy to see how you're progressing toward your goals.

As you begin this journey, if you discover that you need

help connecting your big dreams with specific action items, or if you need to learn how to dream big and set actionable goals for the first time, visit DeniseWalsh.com. There you'll find resources that work with this journal to give you a step-by-step pathway toward the life and relationships you're hoping to have.

My dream is for you to feel immense joy and live your dream life in every way, every day! Make this journal part of your daily routine, and it will give you the space to grow personally, stay on track toward your dreams, see real progress in your relationships, and break through whatever ceiling is holding you back.

It's time for you to enjoy the journey, my friends. Enjoy today!

Day
1

Only I can

change

my life.

No one

can do it for me.

Carol Burnett

Prayer

Thank You, God, for Your amazing power and work within my life. Thank You for the love that surrounds me every day. Thank You for being with me and for guiding every decision I make. Please give me the courage to do what is right, remind me of all the people in my life who care, and help me to love myself every day.

Eyes Wide Open

Take a few moments to consider how God has made His presence known in your life lately. What prayers has He answered for you? How have you experienced Him in your life or surroundings? Write down what is going well for you right now.

_____

_____

_____

_____

_____

_____

_____

_____

Gratitude Game

All About Me

Loving who you are starts with knowing who you are! Answer the following questions as you begin this journey of personal discovery.

How old am I?_____

Something that comes naturally to me is _____
_____.

My favorite word or saying is _____.

My favorite place is _____because
_____.

I think I am super good at _____
_____.

I have some great friends, including _____
_____.

A few things I love to do for fun are _____
_____.

One thing that brings me joy is _____
_____.

One thing I am interested in learning more about is _____
_____
_____.

One goal I want to accomplish over the next thirty days is
_____
_____
_____
_____.

Time to Pray

This is a special place of hope, victory, and healing. It is your opportunity to ask the Holy Spirit to move in certain situations or relationships. Rather than filing your complaints, tell Him how you'd like these situations and relationships to look. Jot down four specific requests below, thanking God as if they have already happened.

1 _____
_____
_____

2 _____
_____
_____

3 _____
_____
_____

4 _____
_____
_____

Time to Listen

You asked the Holy Spirit to move. Now listen to God's voice. You can add music or keep it silent. Take a few deep breaths, close your eyes, relax your body, and slow your mind. Make it a goal to sit in silence, breathing deeply, for five to ten minutes each day.

Time to Write

Did you sense God speaking to you? What do you believe He is calling you to do? Do you feel excited? Conflicted? Peaceful? Did anyone come to mind? Did you get a new idea? Now is the time to write it all down!

_____

_____

_____

_____

_____

_____

_____

_____

_____

_____

_____

_____

_____

_____

_____

_____

_____

_____

Dream Life Goal

Writing your goal down each and every day creates momentum over time. Use this space to write down your current Dream Life Goal as you focus on making progress in one area of life at a time.

_____

_____

_____

_____

_____

Say It

Daily affirmations are simple, positive statements declaring specific goals in their completed state. To get started, think about who you will be, how you will feel, and what your life will look like when your goal is complete. Then write down the affirmations that correspond to the person you are becoming and the life you are creating. A few examples are: I am compassionate to myself and others. I am proud of who I am and who I am becoming. I am grateful for my personal strengths. (Turn to page 246 for a longer list of examples you can choose from.)

Once you have written down your affirmations, read them out loud. You will do this every day until you truly believe them.

I am _____.

I am _____.

I am _____.

I am _____.

Picture It

Cement your big goal in your mind by picturing yourself achieving it. Take a few deep breaths, and picture what your life will look like when your goal is complete. Notice any new details you can see today.

Do It

Dream Life Goal Action Items

Create a to-do list that is specific to your current goal. Taking action-oriented steps each day will take you one step closer to your goal. Be sure that your actions are small enough to complete in one day, and check them off when they are done!

☐ _____

☐ _____

☐ _____

☐ _____

☐ _____

Relationship Action Items

What can you do today to be more intentional about important relationships? Thank a teacher, parent, or friend? Do something fun for someone you care about? Show kindness to someone during the day?

☐ _____

☐ _____

Health Action Items

What actions will you take to improve your physical health? Is it to increase your water intake? Make more time for exercise? Tweak your menu or your sleep time? Log your progress today on the health tracker at the end of the book.

Day
2

It takes
guts
to be
kind.

The Smiths

Prayer

Thank You, God, for Your amazing power and work within my life. Thank You for the love that surrounds me every day. Thank You for being with me and for guiding every decision I make. Please give me the courage to do what is right, remind me of all the people in my life who care, and help me to love myself every day.

Eyes Wide Open

Take a few moments to consider how God has made His presence known in your life lately. What prayers has He answered for you? How have you experienced Him in your life or surroundings? Write down what is going well for you right now.

_____

_____

_____

_____

_____

_____

_____

_____

Gratitude Game

My Superpowers

Good news! You are exactly who you are supposed to be! Circle the character traits that you believe represent who you are. Below, write the positive impact of those attributes. (For example, "Because I am outgoing, I make new friends easily."

"Because I am honest, my family and friends consider me trustworthy.")

I am kind.	I am honest.
I am calm.	I am a finisher.
I am clever.	I am energetic.
I am approachable.	I am athletic.
I am ambitious.	I am flexible.
I am courageous.	I am innovative.
I am hilarious.	I am a good friend.
I am others-focused.	I am a hard worker.
I am organized.	I am creative.
I am patient.	I am studious.

_____

_____

_____

_____

_____

_____

_____

_____

_____

Time to Pray

This is a special place of hope, victory, and healing. It is your opportunity to ask the Holy Spirit to move in certain situations or relationships. Rather than filing your complaints, tell Him how you'd like these situations and relationships to look. Jot down four specific requests below, thanking God as if they have already happened.

1 _____

_____

_____

2 _____

_____

_____

3 _____

_____

_____

4 _____

_____

_____

Time to Listen

You asked the Holy Spirit to move. Now listen to God's voice. You can add music or keep it silent. Take a few deep breaths, close your eyes, relax your body, and slow your mind. Make it a goal to sit in silence, breathing deeply, for five to ten minutes each day.

Time to Write

Did you sense God speaking to you? What do you believe He is calling you to do? Do you feel excited? Conflicted? Peaceful? Did anyone come to mind? Did you get a new idea? Now is the time to write it all down!

_____

_____

_____

_____

_____

_____

_____

_____

_____

_____

_____

_____

_____

_____

_____

_____

_____

_____

Dream Life Goal

Writing your goal down each and every day creates momentum over time. Use this space to write down your current Dream Life Goal as you focus on making progress in one area of life at a time.

_____

_____

_____

_____

_____

Say It

Who will you be, how will you feel, and what will your life look like when your goal is complete? Write down the affirmations that correspond to the person you are becoming and the life you are creating. When you're done, read these affirmations out loud to yourself. (Remember to check out the list of affirmations on page 246 for ideas.)

I am _____.

I am _____.

I am _____.

I am _____.

Picture It

Cement your big goal in your mind by picturing yourself achieving it. Take a few deep breaths, and picture what your life will look like when your goal is complete. Notice any new details you can see today.

Do It

Dream Life Goal Action Items

Create a to-do list that is specific to your current goal. Taking action-oriented steps each day will take you one step closer to your goal. Be sure that your actions are small enough to complete in one day, and check them off when they are done!

☐ _____

☐ _____

☐ _____

☐ _____

☐ _____

Relationship Action Items

What can you do today to be more intentional about important relationships? Thank a teacher, parent, or friend? Do something fun for someone you care about? Show kindness to someone during the day?

☐ _____

☐ _____

Health Action Items

What actions will you take to improve your physical health? Is it to increase your water intake? Make more time for exercise? Tweak your menu or your sleep time? Log your progress today on the health tracker at the end of the book.

**Day
3**

Sometimes
you

win;

sometimes
you

learn.

John C. Maxwell

Prayer

Thank You, God, for Your amazing power and work within my life. Thank You for the love that surrounds me every day. Thank You for being with me and for guiding every decision I make. Please give me the courage to do what is right, remind me of all the people in my life who care, and help me to love myself every day.

Eyes Wide Open

Take a few moments to consider how God has made His presence known in your life lately. What prayers has He answered for you? How have you experienced Him in your life or surroundings? Write down what is going well for you right now.

_____

_____

_____

_____

_____

_____

_____

Gratitude Game

Pivotal Moments

Think about your three greatest successes or most important moments thus far. These can be things you accomplished or completed, or something important that you experienced within your family.

Describe them:

_____

_____

_____

These were important because:

_____

_____

_____

I am proud of myself because:
(Circle all that apply.)

   I worked hard.

   I asked for help.

   I tried something new.

   I helped someone.

   I believed in myself.

   I grew.

_____

_____

_____

Time to Pray

This is a special place of hope, victory, and healing. It is your opportunity to ask the Holy Spirit to move in certain situations or relationships. Rather than filing your complaints, tell Him how you'd like these situations and relationships to look. Jot down four specific requests below, thanking God as if they have already happened.

1 _____
_____
_____

2 _____
_____
_____

3 _____
_____
_____

4 _____
_____
_____

Time to Listen

You asked the Holy Spirit to move. Now listen to God's voice. You can add music or keep it silent. Take a few deep breaths, close your eyes, relax your body, and slow your mind. Make it a goal to sit in silence, breathing deeply, for five to ten minutes each day.

Time to Write

Did you sense God speaking to you? What do you believe He is calling you to do? Do you feel excited? Conflicted? Peaceful? Did anyone come to mind? Did you get a new idea? Now is the time to write it all down!

_____

_____

_____

_____

_____

_____

_____

_____

_____

_____

_____

_____

_____

_____

_____

_____

_____

_____

Dream Life Goal

Writing your goal down each and every day creates momentum over time. Use this space to write down your current Dream Life Goal as you focus on making progress in one area of life at a time.

_____

_____

_____

_____

_____

Say It

Who will you be, how will you feel, and what will your life look like when your goal is complete? Write down the affirmations that correspond to the person you are becoming and the life you are creating. When you're done, read these affirmations out loud to yourself. (Remember to check out the list of affirmations on page 246 for ideas.)

I am _____.

I am _____.

I am _____.

I am _____.

Picture It

Cement your big goal in your mind by picturing yourself achieving it. Take a few deep breaths, and picture what your life will look like when your goal is complete. Notice any new details you can see today.

Do It

Dream Life Goal Action Items

Create a to-do list that is specific to your current goal. Taking action-oriented steps each day will take you one step closer to your goal. Be sure that your actions are small enough to complete in one day, and check them off when they are done!

- ☐ _____
- ☐ _____
- ☐ _____
- ☐ _____
- ☐ _____

Relationship Action Items

What can you do today to be more intentional about important relationships? Thank a teacher, parent, or friend? Do something fun for someone you care about? Show kindness to someone during the day?

- ☐ _____
- ☐ _____

Health Action Items

What actions will you take to improve your physical health? Is it to increase your water intake? Make more time for exercise? Tweak your menu or your sleep time? Log your progress today on the health tracker at the end of the book.

Day
4

No one
looks stupid
when they
are
having fun!

Amy Poehler

Prayer

Thank You, God, for Your amazing power and work within my life. Thank You for the love that surrounds me every day. Thank You for being with me and for guiding every decision I make. Please give me the courage to do what is right, remind me of all the people in my life who care, and help me to love myself every day.

Eyes Wide Open

Take a few moments to consider how God has made His presence known in your life lately. What prayers has He answered for you? How have you experienced Him in your life or surroundings? Write down what is going well for you right now.

_____

_____

_____

_____

_____

_____

_____

_____

Gratitude Game

What Do I Want?

Knowing what you want is half the battle. Once you have a clear vision for what you want your life to look like, you can then start taking steps toward it. Begin by asking yourself, "What do I want?" Write down your answers. Then ask yourself the same question again, and write down anything new that comes up. Do this over and over again until there is nothing new to write.

Once you have created your list, ask yourself what you can add to your calendar today to begin working toward the things you want.

_____

_____

_____

_____

_____

_____

_____

_____

_____

_____

_____

_____

_____

_____

_____

_____

_____

_____

Time to Pray

This is a special place of hope, victory, and healing. It is your opportunity to ask the Holy Spirit to move in certain situations or relationships. Rather than filing your complaints, tell Him how you'd like these situations and relationships to look. Jot down four specific requests below, thanking God as if they have already happened.

1 _____

_____

_____

2 _____

_____

_____

3 _____

_____

_____

4 _____

_____

_____

Time to Listen

You asked the Holy Spirit to move. Now listen to God's voice. You can add music or keep it silent. Take a few deep breaths, close your eyes, relax your body, and slow your mind. Make it a goal to sit in silence, breathing deeply, for five to ten minutes each day.

Time to Write

Did you sense God speaking to you? What do you believe He is calling you to do? Do you feel excited? Conflicted? Peaceful? Did anyone come to mind? Did you get a new idea? Now is the time to write it all down!

_____

_____

_____

_____

_____

_____

_____

_____

_____

_____

_____

_____

_____

_____

_____

_____

_____

_____

_____

Dream Life Goal

Writing your goal down each and every day creates momentum over time. Use this space to write down your current Dream Life Goal as you focus on making progress in one area of life at a time.

_____

_____

_____

_____

_____

Say It

Who will you be, how will you feel, and what will your life look like when your goal is complete? Write down the affirmations that correspond to the person you are becoming and the life you are creating. When you're done, read these affirmations out loud to yourself. (Remember to check out the list of affirmations on page 246 for ideas.)

I am _____.

I am _____.

I am _____.

I am _____.

Picture It

Cement your big goal in your mind by picturing yourself achieving it. Take a few deep breaths, and picture what your life will look like when your goal is complete. Notice any new details you can see today.

Do It

Dream Life Goal Action Items

Create a to-do list that is specific to your current goal. Taking action-oriented steps each day will take you one step closer to your goal. Be sure that your actions are small enough to complete in one day, and check them off when they are done!

☐ _____

☐ _____

☐ _____

☐ _____

☐ _____

Relationship Action Items

What can you do today to be more intentional about important relationships? Thank a teacher, parent, or friend? Do something fun for someone you care about? Show kindness to someone during the day?

☐ _____

☐ _____

Health Action Items

What actions will you take to improve your physical health? Is it to increase your water intake? Make more time for exercise? Tweak your menu or your sleep time? Log your progress today on the health tracker at the end of the book.

Believe you

can

and you are

halfway

there.

Theodore Roosevelt

Prayer

Thank You, God, for Your amazing power and work within my life. Thank You for the love that surrounds me every day. Thank You for being with me and for guiding every decision I make. Please give me the courage to do what is right, remind me of all the people in my life who care, and help me to love myself every day.

Eyes Wide Open

Take a few moments to consider how God has made His presence known in your life lately. What prayers has He answered for you? How have you experienced Him in your life or surroundings? Write down what is going well for you right now.

_____

_____

_____

_____

_____

_____

_____

_____

Gratitude Game

That Finish Line Feeling

Describe a time you were scared to do something but completed it anyway. How did you feel before, during, and after that experience? Write about the feeling you had when you completed the hard thing.

Time to Pray

This is a special place of hope, victory, and healing. It is your opportunity to ask the Holy Spirit to move in certain situations or relationships. Rather than filing your complaints, tell Him how you'd like these situations and relationships to look. Jot down four specific requests below, thanking God as if they have already happened.

1 _____

_____

_____

2 _____

_____

_____

3 _____

_____

_____

4 _____

_____

_____

Time to Listen

You asked the Holy Spirit to move. Now listen to God's voice. You can add music or keep it silent. Take a few deep breaths, close your eyes, relax your body, and slow your mind. Make it a goal to sit in silence, breathing deeply, for five to ten minutes each day.

Time to Write

Did you sense God speaking to you? What do you believe He is calling you to do? Do you feel excited? Conflicted? Peaceful? Did anyone come to mind? Did you get a new idea? Now is the time to write it all down!

_____

_____

_____

_____

_____

_____

_____

_____

_____

_____

_____

_____

_____

_____

_____

_____

_____

_____

Dream Life Goal

Writing your goal down each and every day creates momentum over time. Use this space to write down your current Dream Life Goal as you focus on making progress in one area of life at a time.

_____

_____

_____

_____

_____

Say It

Who will you be, how will you feel, and what will your life look like when your goal is complete? Write down the affirmations that correspond to the person you are becoming and the life you are creating. When you're done, read these affirmations out loud to yourself. (Remember to check out the list of affirmations on page 246 for ideas.)

I am _____,

I am _____,

I am _____,

I am _____,

Picture It

Cement your big goal in your mind by picturing yourself achieving it. Take a few deep breaths, and picture what your life will look like when your goal is complete. Notice any new details you can see today.

Do It

Dream Life Goal Action Items

Create a to-do list that is specific to your current goal. Taking action-oriented steps each day will take you one step closer to your goal. Be sure that your actions are small enough to complete in one day, and check them off when they are done!

- ☐ _____
- ☐ _____
- ☐ _____
- ☐ _____
- ☐ _____

Relationship Action Items

What can you do today to be more intentional about important relationships? Thank a teacher, parent, or friend? Do something fun for someone you care about? Show kindness to someone during the day?

- ☐ _____
- ☐ _____

Health Action Items

What actions will you take to improve your physical health? Is it to increase your water intake? Make more time for exercise? Tweak your menu or your sleep time? Log your progress today on the health tracker at the end of the book.

Family:

a little bit

loud,

a little bit

crazy,

and a whole lot of

love.

Prayer

Thank You, God, for Your amazing power and work within my life. Thank You for the love that surrounds me every day. Thank You for being with me and for guiding every decision I make. Please give me the courage to do what is right, remind me of all the people in my life who care, and help me to love myself every day.

Eyes Wide Open

Take a few moments to consider how God has made His presence known in your life lately. What prayers has He answered for you? How have you experienced Him in your life or surroundings? Write down what is going well for you right now.

_____

_____

_____

_____

_____

_____

_____

Gratitude Game

Everyday Staycation

What are some of the best things about your home? What do you like to do the most when you are there? Write about your favorite space in your home to relax and be yourself.

Time to Pray

This is a special place of hope, victory, and healing. It is your opportunity to ask the Holy Spirit to move in certain situations or relationships. Rather than filing your complaints, tell Him how you'd like these situations and relationships to look. Jot down four specific requests below, thanking God as if they have already happened.

1 _____

_____

_____

2 _____

_____

_____

3 _____

_____

_____

4 _____

_____

_____

Time to Listen

You asked the Holy Spirit to move. Now listen to God's voice. You can add music or keep it silent. Take a few deep breaths, close your eyes, relax your body, and slow your mind. Make it a goal to sit in silence, breathing deeply, for five to ten minutes each day.

Time to Write

Did you sense God speaking to you? What do you believe He is calling you to do? Do you feel excited? Conflicted? Peaceful? Did anyone come to mind? Did you get a new idea? Now is the time to write it all down!

_____

_____

_____

_____

_____

_____

_____

_____

_____

_____

_____

_____

_____

_____

_____

_____

_____

_____

_____

Dream Life Goal

Writing your goal down each and every day creates momentum over time. Use this space to write down your current Dream Life Goal as you focus on making progress in one area of life at a time.

_____

_____

_____

_____

_____

Say It

Who will you be, how will you feel, and what will your life look like when your goal is complete? Write down the affirmations that correspond to the person you are becoming and the life you are creating. When you're done, read these affirmations out loud to yourself. (Remember to check out the list of affirmations on page 246 for ideas.)

I am _____.

I am _____.

I am _____.

I am _____.

Picture It

Cement your big goal in your mind by picturing yourself achieving it. Take a few deep breaths, and picture what your life will look like when your goal is complete. Notice any new details you can see today.

Do It

Dream Life Goal Action Items

Create a to-do list that is specific to your current goal. Taking action-oriented steps each day will take you one step closer to your goal. Be sure that your actions are small enough to complete in one day, and check them off when they are done!

- ☐ _____
- ☐ _____
- ☐ _____
- ☐ _____
- ☐ _____

Relationship Action Items

What can you do today to be more intentional about important relationships? Thank a teacher, parent, or friend? Do something fun for someone you care about? Show kindness to someone during the day?

- ☐ _____
- ☐ _____

Health Action Items

What actions will you take to improve your physical health? Is it to increase your water intake? Make more time for exercise? Tweak your menu or your sleep time? Log your progress today on the health tracker at the end of the book.

Things are never quite

as scary

when you've got a

best friend.

Bill Watterson, Calvin and Hobbes

Prayer

Thank You, God, for Your amazing power and work within my life. Thank You for the love that surrounds me every day. Thank You for being with me and for guiding every decision I make. Please give me the courage to do what is right, remind me of all the people in my life who care, and help me to love myself every day.

Eyes Wide Open

Take a few moments to consider how God has made His presence known in your life lately. What prayers has He answered for you? How have you experienced Him in your life or surroundings? Write down what is going well for you right now.

_____

_____

_____

_____

_____

_____

Gratitude Game

BFF

Name several of your good friends. What do you enjoy about being with them? Why do you trust them? What fun things do you do together? How do you feel when you are around them? How do they encourage your dreams? How do they help you avoid drama?

Time to Pray

This is a special place of hope, victory, and healing. It is your opportunity to ask the Holy Spirit to move in certain situations or relationships. Rather than filing your complaints, tell Him how you'd like these situations and relationships to look. Jot down four specific requests below, thanking God as if they have already happened.

1 _____

_____

_____

2 _____

_____

_____

3 _____

_____

_____

4 _____

_____

_____

Time to Listen

You asked the Holy Spirit to move. Now listen to God's voice. You can add music or keep it silent. Take a few deep breaths, close your eyes, relax your body, and slow your mind. Make it a goal to sit in silence, breathing deeply, for five to ten minutes each day.

Time to Write

Did you sense God speaking to you? What do you believe He is calling you to do? Do you feel excited? Conflicted? Peaceful? Did anyone come to mind? Did you get a new idea? Now is the time to write it all down!

_____

_____

_____

_____

_____

_____

_____

_____

_____

_____

_____

_____

_____

_____

_____

_____

_____

_____

Dream Life Goal

Writing your goal down each and every day creates momentum over time. Use this space to write down your current Dream Life Goal as you focus on making progress in one area of life at a time.

_____

_____

_____

_____

_____

Say It

Who will you be, how will you feel, and what will your life look like when your goal is complete? Write down the affirmations that correspond to the person you are becoming and the life you are creating. When you're done, read these affirmations out loud to yourself. (Remember to check out the list of affirmations on page 246 for ideas.)

I am _____.

I am _____.

I am _____.

I am _____.

Picture It

Cement your big goal in your mind by picturing yourself achieving it. Take a few deep breaths, and picture what your life will look like when your goal is complete. Notice any new details you can see today.

Do It

Dream Life Goal Action Items

Create a to-do list that is specific to your current goal. Taking action-oriented steps each day will take you one step closer to your goal. Be sure that your actions are small enough to complete in one day, and check them off when they are done!

- [ ] _____
- [ ] _____
- [ ] _____
- [ ] _____
- [ ] _____

Relationship Action Items

What can you do today to be more intentional about important relationships? Thank a teacher, parent, or friend? Do something fun for someone you care about? Show kindness to someone during the day?

- [ ] _____
- [ ] _____

Health Action Items

What actions will you take to improve your physical health? Is it to increase your water intake? Make more time for exercise? Tweak your menu or your sleep time? Log your progress today on the health tracker at the end of the book.

Far too many
people are

looking

for the right person,
instead of

trying to be

the right person.

Gloria Steinem

Prayer

Thank You, God, for Your amazing power and work within my life. Thank You for the love that surrounds me every day. Thank You for being with me and for guiding every decision I make. Please give me the courage to do what is right, remind me of all the people in my life who care, and help me to love myself every day.

Eyes Wide Open

Take a few moments to consider how God has made His presence known in your life lately. What prayers has He answered for you? How have you experienced Him in your life or surroundings? Write down what is going well for you right now.

_____

_____

_____

_____

_____

_____

_____

Gratitude Game

Write It Out

Think of something that is currently bothering you. Write about the situation without trying to solve it. Just focus on getting your thoughts out of your mind and onto paper. End your writing with three things that are going well in your life even though something hard is happening too.

1 _____

2 _____

3 _____

Time to Pray

This is a special place of hope, victory, and healing. It is your opportunity to ask the Holy Spirit to move in certain situations or relationships. Rather than filing your complaints, tell Him how you'd like these situations and relationships to look. Jot down four specific requests below, thanking God as if they have already happened.

1 _____

_____

_____

2 _____

_____

_____

3 _____

_____

_____

4 _____

_____

_____

Time to Listen

You asked the Holy Spirit to move. Now listen to God's voice. You can add music or keep it silent. Take a few deep breaths, close your eyes, relax your body, and slow your mind. Make it a goal to sit in silence, breathing deeply, for five to ten minutes each day.

Time to Write

Did you sense God speaking to you? What do you believe He is calling you to do? Do you feel excited? Conflicted? Peaceful? Did anyone come to mind? Did you get a new idea? Now is the time to write it all down!

_____

_____

_____

_____

_____

_____

_____

_____

_____

_____

_____

_____

_____

_____

_____

_____

_____

Dream Life Goal

Writing your goal down each and every day creates momentum over time. Use this space to write down your current Dream Life Goal as you focus on making progress in one area of life at a time.

_____

_____

_____

_____

_____

Say It

Who will you be, how will you feel, and what will your life look like when your goal is complete? Write down the affirmations that correspond to the person you are becoming and the life you are creating. When you're done, read these affirmations out loud to yourself. (Remember to check out the list of affirmations on page 246 for ideas.)

I am _____.

I am _____.

I am _____.

I am _____.

Picture It

Cement your big goal in your mind by picturing yourself achieving it. Take a few deep breaths, and picture what your life will look like when your goal is complete. Notice any new details you can see today.

Do It

Dream Life Goal Action Items

Create a to-do list that is specific to your current goal. Taking action-oriented steps each day will take you one step closer to your goal. Be sure that your actions are small enough to complete in one day, and check them off when they are done!

☐ _____

☐ _____

☐ _____

☐ _____

☐ _____

Relationship Action Items

What can you do today to be more intentional about important relationships? Thank a teacher, parent, or friend? Do something fun for someone you care about? Show kindness to someone during the day?

☐ _____

☐ _____

Health Action Items

What actions will you take to improve your physical health? Is it to increase your water intake? Make more time for exercise? Tweak your menu or your sleep time? Log your progress today on the health tracker at the end of the book.

Day
9

I

can

do

hard things.

Jennifer Nettles

Prayer

Thank You, God, for Your amazing power and work within my life. Thank You for the love that surrounds me every day. Thank You for being with me and for guiding every decision I make. Please give me the courage to do what is right, remind me of all the people in my life who care, and help me to love myself every day.

Eyes Wide Open

Take a few moments to consider how God has made His presence known in your life lately. What prayers has He answered for you? How have you experienced Him in your life or surroundings? Write down what is going well for you right now.

_____

_____

_____

_____

_____

_____

_____

Gratitude Game

Words to My Younger Self

What words of wisdom would you give to your ten-year-old self about life, relationships, school, or hobbies? Write a letter to your ten-year-old self in the space provided.

Time to Pray

This is a special place of hope, victory, and healing. It is your opportunity to ask the Holy Spirit to move in certain situations or relationships. Rather than filing your complaints, tell Him how you'd like these situations and relationships to look. Jot down four specific requests below, thanking God as if they have already happened.

1 _____

_____

2 _____

_____

3 _____

_____

4 _____

_____

Time to Listen

You asked the Holy Spirit to move. Now listen to God's voice. You can add music or keep it silent. Take a few deep breaths, close your eyes, relax your body, and slow your mind. Make it a goal to sit in silence, breathing deeply, for five to ten minutes each day.

Time to Write

Did you sense God speaking to you? What do you believe He is calling you to do? Do you feel excited? Conflicted? Peaceful? Did anyone come to mind? Did you get a new idea? Now is the time to write it all down!

_____

_____

_____

_____

_____

_____

_____

_____

_____

_____

_____

_____

_____

_____

_____

_____

_____

_____

_____

Dream Life Goal

Writing your goal down each and every day creates momentum over time. Use this space to write down your current Dream Life Goal as you focus on making progress in one area of life at a time.

_____

_____

_____

_____

_____

Say It

Who will you be, how will you feel, and what will your life look like when your goal is complete? Write down the affirmations that correspond to the person you are becoming and the life you are creating. When you're done, read these affirmations out loud to yourself. (Remember to check out the list of affirmations on page 246 for ideas.)

I am _____.

I am _____.

I am _____.

I am _____.

Picture It

Cement your big goal in your mind by picturing yourself achieving it. Take a few deep breaths, and picture what your life will look like when your goal is complete. Notice any new details you can see today.

Do It

Dream Life Goal Action Items

Create a to-do list that is specific to your current goal. Taking action-oriented steps each day will take you one step closer to your goal. Be sure that your actions are small enough to complete in one day, and check them off when they are done!

- [ ] _____
- [ ] _____
- [ ] _____
- [ ] _____
- [ ] _____

Relationship Action Items

What can you do today to be more intentional about important relationships? Thank a teacher, parent, or friend? Do something fun for someone you care about? Show kindness to someone during the day?

- [ ] _____
- [ ] _____

Health Action Items

What actions will you take to improve your physical health? Is it to increase your water intake? Make more time for exercise? Tweak your menu or your sleep time? Log your progress today on the health tracker at the end of the book.

Day
10

Mistakes
are
proof
that you are
trying.

Jennifer Lim

73

Prayer

Thank You, God, for Your amazing power and work within my life. Thank You for the love that surrounds me every day. Thank You for being with me and for guiding every decision I make. Please give me the courage to do what is right, remind me of all the people in my life who care, and help me to love myself every day.

Eyes Wide Open

Take a few moments to consider how God has made His presence known in your life lately. What prayers has He answered for you? How have you experienced Him in your life or surroundings? Write down what is going well for you right now.

_____

_____

_____

_____

_____

_____

_____

_____

Gratitude Game

Failing Forward

Name a time when you made a mistake or feel like you messed up. Describe what happened. At the time, were you able to see God with you in the situation? Where do you see His presence in it now? What did you learn from it? How could you have handled the situation differently?

_____

_____

_____

_____

_____

_____

_____

_____

_____

_____

_____

_____

_____

_____

_____

_____

_____

_____

Time to Pray

This is a special place of hope, victory, and healing. It is your opportunity to ask the Holy Spirit to move in certain situations or relationships. Rather than filing your complaints, tell Him how you'd like these situations and relationships to look. Jot down four specific requests below, thanking God as if they have already happened.

1 _____

_____

_____

2 _____

_____

_____

3 _____

_____

_____

4 _____

_____

_____

Time to Listen

You asked the Holy Spirit to move. Now listen to God's voice. You can add music or keep it silent. Take a few deep breaths, close your eyes, relax your body, and slow your mind. Make it a goal to sit in silence, breathing deeply, for five to ten minutes each day.

Time to Write

Did you sense God speaking to you? What do you believe He is calling you to do? Do you feel excited? Conflicted? Peaceful? Did anyone come to mind? Did you get a new idea? Now is the time to write it all down!

_____

_____

_____

_____

_____

_____

_____

_____

_____

_____

_____

_____

_____

_____

_____

_____

_____

_____

_____

Dream Life Goal

Writing your goal down each and every day creates momentum over time. Use this space to write down your current Dream Life Goal as you focus on making progress in one area of life at a time.

_____

_____

_____

_____

_____

Say It

Who will you be, how will you feel, and what will your life look like when your goal is complete? Write down the affirmations that correspond to the person you are becoming and the life you are creating. When you're done, read these affirmations out loud to yourself. (Remember to check out the list of affirmations on page 246 for ideas.)

I am _____.

I am _____.

I am _____.

I am _____.

Picture It

Cement your big goal in your mind by picturing yourself achieving it. Take a few deep breaths, and picture what your life will look like when your goal is complete. Notice any new details you can see today.

Do It

Dream Life Goal Action Items

Create a to-do list that is specific to your current goal. Taking action-oriented steps each day will take you one step closer to your goal. Be sure that your actions are small enough to complete in one day, and check them off when they are done!

- [ ] _____
- [ ] _____
- [ ] _____
- [ ] _____
- [ ] _____

Relationship Action Items

What can you do today to be more intentional about important relationships? Thank a teacher, parent, or friend? Do something fun for someone you care about? Show kindness to someone during the day?

- [ ] _____
- [ ] _____

Health Action Items

What actions will you take to improve your physical health? Is it to increase your water intake? Make more time for exercise? Tweak your menu or your sleep time? Log your progress today on the health tracker at the end of the book.

Don't be a
victim of

self-talk.

Remember, you
are

listening.

Bob Proctor

Prayer

Thank You, God, for Your amazing power and work within my life. Thank You for the love that surrounds me every day. Thank You for being with me and for guiding every decision I make. Please give me the courage to do what is right, remind me of all the people in my life who care, and help me to love myself every day.

Eyes Wide Open

Take a few moments to consider how God has made His presence known in your life lately. What prayers has He answered for you? How have you experienced Him in your life or surroundings? Write down what is going well for you right now.

_____

_____

_____

_____

_____

_____

_____

Gratitude Game

Taking Care of Myself

Name three things that you do to feel good about yourself, take care of your physical body, or recharge and how often you do them. How do these actions and activities improve your physical, mental/emotional, and spiritual health? How do these self-care practices improve your relationships?

Time to Pray

This is a special place of hope, victory, and healing. It is your opportunity to ask the Holy Spirit to move in certain situations or relationships. Rather than filing your complaints, tell Him how you'd like these situations and relationships to look. Jot down four specific requests below, thanking God as if they have already happened.

1 _____

_____

_____

2 _____

_____

_____

3 _____

_____

_____

4 _____

_____

_____

Time to Listen

You asked the Holy Spirit to move. Now listen to God's voice. You can add music or keep it silent. Take a few deep breaths, close your eyes, relax your body, and slow your mind. Make it a goal to sit in silence, breathing deeply, for five to ten minutes each day.

Time to Write

Did you sense God speaking to you? What do you believe He is calling you to do? Do you feel excited? Conflicted? Peaceful? Did anyone come to mind? Did you get a new idea? Now is the time to write it all down!

_____

_____

_____

_____

_____

_____

_____

_____

_____

_____

_____

_____

_____

_____

_____

_____

_____

_____

_____

Dream Life Goal

Writing your goal down each and every day creates momentum over time. Use this space to write down your current Dream Life Goal as you focus on making progress in one area of life at a time.

_____

_____

_____

_____

_____

Say It

Who will you be, how will you feel, and what will your life look like when your goal is complete? Write down the affirmations that correspond to the person you are becoming and the life you are creating. When you're done, read these affirmations out loud to yourself. (Remember to check out the list of affirmations on page 246 for ideas.)

I am _____.

I am _____.

I am _____.

I am _____.

Picture It

Cement your big goal in your mind by picturing yourself achieving it. Take a few deep breaths, and picture what your life will look like when your goal is complete. Notice any new details you can see today.

Do It

Dream Life Goal Action Items

Create a to-do list that is specific to your current goal. Taking action-oriented steps each day will take you one step closer to your goal. Be sure that your actions are small enough to complete in one day, and check them off when they are done!

☐ _____

☐ _____

☐ _____

☐ _____

☐ _____

Relationship Action Items

What can you do today to be more intentional about important relationships? Thank a teacher, parent, or friend? Do something fun for someone you care about? Show kindness to someone during the day?

☐ _____

☐ _____

Health Action Items

What actions will you take to improve your physical health? Is it to increase your water intake? Make more time for exercise? Tweak your menu or your sleep time? Log your progress today on the health tracker at the end of the book.

Day
12

Share your
smile
with the world.
It's a symbol of

friendship
and
peace.

Christie Brinkley

Prayer

Thank You, God, for Your amazing power and work within my life. Thank You for the love that surrounds me every day. Thank You for being with me and for guiding every decision I make. Please give me the courage to do what is right, remind me of all the people in my life who care, and help me to love myself every day.

Eyes Wide Open

Take a few moments to consider how God has made His presence known in your life lately. What prayers has He answered for you? How have you experienced Him in your life or surroundings? Write down what is going well for you right now.

Gratitude Game

Problem Solver

There are three ways to solve a problem: accept it, change it, or stay miserable.

Think of a problem you are currently experiencing and which one of these actions could best solve it. Write about how you can accept or change your situation. (This is assuming you do not want to stay miserable.)

_____

_____

_____

_____

_____

_____

_____

_____

_____

_____

_____

_____

_____

_____

_____

_____

_____

_____

_____

_____

_____

_____

Day 12

Time to Pray

This is a special place of hope, victory, and healing. It is your opportunity to ask the Holy Spirit to move in certain situations or relationships. Rather than filing your complaints, tell Him how you'd like these situations and relationships to look. Jot down four specific requests below, thanking God as if they have already happened.

1 _____

_____

_____

2 _____

_____

_____

3 _____

_____

_____

4 _____

_____

_____

Time to Listen

You asked the Holy Spirit to move. Now listen to God's voice. You can add music or keep it silent. Take a few deep breaths, close your eyes, relax your body, and slow your mind. Make it a goal to sit in silence, breathing deeply, for five to ten minutes each day.

Time to Write

Did you sense God speaking to you? What do you believe He is calling you to do? Do you feel excited? Conflicted? Peaceful? Did anyone come to mind? Did you get a new idea? Now is the time to write it all down!

_____

_____

_____

_____

_____

_____

_____

_____

_____

_____

_____

_____

_____

_____

_____

_____

_____

_____

Dream Life Goal

Writing your goal down each and every day creates momentum over time. Use this space to write down your current Dream Life Goal as you focus on making progress in one area of life at a time.

_____

_____

_____

_____

_____

Say It

Who will you be, how will you feel, and what will your life look like when your goal is complete? Write down the affirmations that correspond to the person you are becoming and the life you are creating. When you're done, read these affirmations out loud to yourself. (Remember to check out the list of affirmations on page 246 for ideas.)

I am _____.

I am _____.

I am _____.

I am _____.

Picture It

Cement your big goal in your mind by picturing yourself achieving it. Take a few deep breaths, and picture what your life will look like when your goal is complete. Notice any new details you can see today.

Do It

Dream Life Goal Action Items

Create a to-do list that is specific to your current goal. Taking action-oriented steps each day will take you one step closer to your goal. Be sure that your actions are small enough to complete in one day, and check them off when they are done!

- [ ] _____
- [ ] _____
- [ ] _____
- [ ] _____
- [ ] _____

Relationship Action Items

What can you do today to be more intentional about important relationships? Thank a teacher, parent, or friend? Do something fun for someone you care about? Show kindness to someone during the day?

- [ ] _____
- [ ] _____

Health Action Items

What actions will you take to improve your physical health? Is it to increase your water intake? Make more time for exercise? Tweak your menu or your sleep time? Log your progress today on the health tracker at the end of the book.

Day
13

The

secret

of getting ahead is

getting started.

Mark Twain

Prayer

Thank You, God, for Your amazing power and work within my life. Thank You for the love that surrounds me every day. Thank You for being with me and for guiding every decision I make. Please give me the courage to do what is right, remind me of all the people in my life who care, and help me to love myself every day.

Eyes Wide Open

Take a few moments to consider how God has made His presence known in your life lately. What prayers has He answered for you? How have you experienced Him in your life or surroundings? Write down what is going well for you right now.

_____

_____

_____

_____

_____

_____

_____

Gratitude Game

Fear Slasher

We experience fear and anxiety when we think bad or unpleasant things will happen in our future. The funny thing is that they often *don't* happen, and we are worrying for no reason! Today if you are worried or anxious, take a deep breath and ask yourself, "What is true in my life?" Write about all things that are true for you in the reflection below.

Examples: I am loved. I have a safe home. I am a good friend. God loves me. I am worthy and worth it.

_____

_____

_____

_____

_____

_____

_____

_____

_____

_____

_____

_____

_____

_____

_____

_____

_____

_____

Time to Pray

This is a special place of hope, victory, and healing. It is your opportunity to ask the Holy Spirit to move in certain situations or relationships. Rather than filing your complaints, tell Him how you'd like these situations and relationships to look. Jot down four specific requests below, thanking God as if they have already happened.

1 _____

_____

_____

2 _____

_____

_____

3 _____

_____

_____

4 _____

_____

_____

Time to Listen

You asked the Holy Spirit to move. Now listen to God's voice. You can add music or keep it silent. Take a few deep breaths, close your eyes, relax your body, and slow your mind. Make it a goal to sit in silence, breathing deeply, for five to ten minutes each day.

Time to Write

Did you sense God speaking to you? What do you believe He is calling you to do? Do you feel excited? Conflicted? Peaceful? Did anyone come to mind? Did you get a new idea? Now is the time to write it all down!

_____

_____

_____

_____

_____

_____

_____

_____

_____

_____

_____

_____

_____

_____

_____

_____

_____

_____

Dream Life Goal

Writing your goal down each and every day creates momentum over time. Use this space to write down your current Dream Life Goal as you focus on making progress in one area of life at a time.

_____

_____

_____

_____

_____

Say It

Who will you be, how will you feel, and what will your life look like when your goal is complete? Write down the affirmations that correspond to the person you are becoming and the life you are creating. When you're done, read these affirmations out loud to yourself. (Remember to check out the list of affirmations on page 246 for ideas.)

I am _____.

I am _____.

I am _____.

I am _____.

Picture It

Cement your big goal in your mind by picturing yourself achieving it. Take a few deep breaths, and picture what your life will look like when your goal is complete. Notice any new details you can see today.

Do It

Dream Life Goal Action Items

Create a to-do list that is specific to your current goal. Taking action-oriented steps each day will take you one step closer to your goal. Be sure that your actions are small enough to complete in one day, and check them off when they are done!

☐ _____

☐ _____

☐ _____

☐ _____

☐ _____

Relationship Action Items

What can you do today to be more intentional about important relationships? Thank a teacher, parent, or friend? Do something fun for someone you care about? Show kindness to someone during the day?

☐ _____

☐ _____

Health Action Items

What actions will you take to improve your physical health? Is it to increase your water intake? Make more time for exercise? Tweak your menu or your sleep time? Log your progress today on the health tracker at the end of the book.

Day 14

Do your *best* until *you* make *yourself* proud.

Prayer

Thank You, God, for Your amazing power and work within my life. Thank You for the love that surrounds me every day. Thank You for being with me and for guiding every decision I make. Please give me the courage to do what is right, remind me of all the people in my life who care, and help me to love myself every day.

Eyes Wide Open

Take a few moments to consider how God has made His presence known in your life lately. What prayers has He answered for you? How have you experienced Him in your life or surroundings? Write down what is going well for you right now.

_____

_____

_____

_____

_____

_____

_____

_____

Gratitude Game

Full of Joy

Think about something you love doing. Describe a time when you got to do that thing and felt overwhelmed with joy. Try to add as many details as you can about the experience and the way it made you feel.

Time to Pray

This is a special place of hope, victory, and healing. It is your opportunity to ask the Holy Spirit to move in certain situations or relationships. Rather than filing your complaints, tell Him how you'd like these situations and relationships to look. Jot down four specific requests below, thanking God as if they have already happened.

1 _____

_____

_____

2 _____

_____

_____

3 _____

_____

_____

4 _____

_____

_____

Time to Listen

You asked the Holy Spirit to move. Now listen to God's voice. You can add music or keep it silent. Take a few deep breaths, close your eyes, relax your body, and slow your mind. Make it a goal to sit in silence, breathing deeply, for five to ten minutes each day.

Time to Write

Did you sense God speaking to you? What do you believe He is calling you to do? Do you feel excited? Conflicted? Peaceful? Did anyone come to mind? Did you get a new idea? Now is the time to write it all down!

_____

_____

_____

_____

_____

_____

_____

_____

_____

_____

_____

_____

_____

_____

_____

_____

_____

_____

Dream Life Goal

Writing your goal down each and every day creates momentum over time. Use this space to write down your current Dream Life Goal as you focus on making progress in one area of life at a time.

_____

_____

_____

_____

_____

Say It

Who will you be, how will you feel, and what will your life look like when your goal is complete? Write down the affirmations that correspond to the person you are becoming and the life you are creating. When you're done, read these affirmations out loud to yourself. (Remember to check out the list of affirmations on page 246 for ideas.)

I am _____.

I am _____.

I am _____.

I am _____.

Picture It

Cement your big goal in your mind by picturing yourself achieving it. Take a few deep breaths, and picture what your life will look like when your goal is complete. Notice any new details you can see today.

Do It

Dream Life Goal Action Items

Create a to-do list that is specific to your current goal. Taking action-oriented steps each day will take you one step closer to your goal. Be sure that your actions are small enough to complete in one day, and check them off when they are done!

- [ ] _____
- [ ] _____
- [ ] _____
- [ ] _____
- [ ] _____

Relationship Action Items

What can you do today to be more intentional about important relationships? Thank a teacher, parent, or friend? Do something fun for someone you care about? Show kindness to someone during the day?

- [ ] _____
- [ ] _____

Health Action Items

What actions will you take to improve your physical health? Is it to increase your water intake? Make more time for exercise? Tweak your menu or your sleep time? Log your progress today on the health tracker at the end of the book.

Day
15

People may

*hear your
words,*

but they

*feel your
attitude.*

John C. Maxwell

Prayer

Thank You, God, for Your amazing power and work within my life. Thank You for the love that surrounds me every day. Thank You for being with me and for guiding every decision I make. Please give me the courage to do what is right, remind me of all the people in my life who care, and help me to love myself every day.

Eyes Wide Open

Take a few moments to consider how God has made His presence known in your life lately. What prayers has He answered for you? How have you experienced Him in your life or surroundings? Write down what is going well for you right now.

_____

_____

_____

_____

_____

_____

_____

_____

Gratitude Game

Spread the Love

Name three traits that you would like others to see in you. Why do you want them to see these qualities in you?

Time to Pray

This is a special place of hope, victory, and healing. It is your opportunity to ask the Holy Spirit to move in certain situations or relationships. Rather than filing your complaints, tell Him how you'd like these situations and relationships to look. Jot down four specific requests below, thanking God as if they have already happened.

1 _____

_____

_____

2 _____

_____

_____

3 _____

_____

_____

4 _____

_____

_____

Time to Listen

You asked the Holy Spirit to move. Now listen to God's voice. You can add music or keep it silent. Take a few deep breaths, close your eyes, relax your body, and slow your mind. Make it a goal to sit in silence, breathing deeply, for five to ten minutes each day.

Time to Write

Did you sense God speaking to you? What do you believe He is calling you to do? Do you feel excited? Conflicted? Peaceful? Did anyone come to mind? Did you get a new idea? Now is the time to write it all down!

_____

_____

_____

_____

_____

_____

_____

_____

_____

_____

_____

_____

_____

_____

_____

_____

_____

Dream Life Goal

Writing your goal down each and every day creates momentum over time. Use this space to write down your current Dream Life Goal as you focus on making progress in one area of life at a time.

_____

_____

_____

_____

_____

Say It

Who will you be, how will you feel, and what will your life look like when your goal is complete? Write down the affirmations that correspond to the person you are becoming and the life you are creating. When you're done, read these affirmations out loud to yourself. (Remember to check out the list of affirmations on page 246 for ideas.)

I am _____.

I am _____.

I am _____.

I am _____.

Picture It

Cement your big goal in your mind by picturing yourself achieving it. Take a few deep breaths, and picture what your life will look like when your goal is complete. Notice any new details you can see today.

Do It

Dream Life Goal Action Items

Create a to-do list that is specific to your current goal. Taking action-oriented steps each day will take you one step closer to your goal. Be sure that your actions are small enough to complete in one day, and check them off when they are done!

- [ ] _____
- [ ] _____
- [ ] _____
- [ ] _____
- [ ] _____

Relationship Action Items

What can you do today to be more intentional about important relationships? Thank a teacher, parent, or friend? Do something fun for someone you care about? Show kindness to someone during the day?

- [ ] _____
- [ ] _____

Health Action Items

What actions will you take to improve your physical health? Is it to increase your water intake? Make more time for exercise? Tweak your menu or your sleep time? Log your progress today on the health tracker at the end of the book.

Day
16

Clarity
is
key.

Prayer

Thank You, God, for Your amazing power and work within my life. Thank You for the love that surrounds me every day. Thank You for being with me and for guiding every decision I make. Please give me the courage to do what is right, remind me of all the people in my life who care, and help me to love myself every day.

Eyes Wide Open

Take a few moments to consider how God has made His presence known in your life lately. What prayers has He answered for you? How have you experienced Him in your life or surroundings? Write down what is going well for you right now.

_____

_____

_____

_____

_____

_____

_____

_____

Gratitude Game

Dream Big

Write down fifteen things you want to do or become in your life and fifteen things you want to have.

Time to Pray

This is a special place of hope, victory, and healing. It is your opportunity to ask the Holy Spirit to move in certain situations or relationships. Rather than filing your complaints, tell Him how you'd like these situations and relationships to look. Jot down four specific requests below, thanking God as if they have already happened.

1 _____

_____

_____

2 _____

_____

_____

3 _____

_____

_____

4 _____

_____

_____

Time to Listen

You asked the Holy Spirit to move. Now listen to God's voice. You can add music or keep it silent. Take a few deep breaths, close your eyes, relax your body, and slow your mind. Make it a goal to sit in silence, breathing deeply, for five to ten minutes each day.

Time to Write

Did you sense God speaking to you? What do you believe He is calling you to do? Do you feel excited? Conflicted? Peaceful? Did anyone come to mind? Did you get a new idea? Now is the time to write it all down!

_____

_____

_____

_____

_____

_____

_____

_____

_____

_____

_____

_____

_____

_____

_____

_____

_____

_____

Dream Life Goal

Writing your goal down each and every day creates momentum over time. Use this space to write down your current Dream Life Goal as you focus on making progress in one area of life at a time.

_____

_____

_____

_____

_____

Say It

Who will you be, how will you feel, and what will your life look like when your goal is complete? Write down the affirmations that correspond to the person you are becoming and the life you are creating. When you're done, read these affirmations out loud to yourself. (Remember to check out the list of affirmations on page 246 for ideas.)

I am _____.

I am _____.

I am _____.

I am _____.

Picture It

Cement your big goal in your mind by picturing yourself achieving it. Take a few deep breaths, and picture what your life will look like when your goal is complete. Notice any new details you can see today.

Do It

Dream Life Goal Action Items

Create a to-do list that is specific to your current goal. Taking action-oriented steps each day will take you one step closer to your goal. Be sure that your actions are small enough to complete in one day, and check them off when they are done!

- ☐ _____
- ☐ _____
- ☐ _____
- ☐ _____
- ☐ _____

Relationship Action Items

What can you do today to be more intentional about important relationships? Thank a teacher, parent, or friend? Do something fun for someone you care about? Show kindness to someone during the day?

- ☐ _____
- ☐ _____

Health Action Items

What actions will you take to improve your physical health? Is it to increase your water intake? Make more time for exercise? Tweak your menu or your sleep time? Log your progress today on the health tracker at the end of the book.

A river
cuts through
rock not because
of its
power
but because
of its
persistence.

James Watkins

Prayer

Thank You, God, for Your amazing power and work within my life. Thank You for the love that surrounds me every day. Thank You for being with me and for guiding every decision I make. Please give me the courage to do what is right, remind me of all the people in my life who care, and help me to love myself every day.

Eyes Wide Open

Take a few moments to consider how God has made His presence known in your life lately. What prayers has He answered for you? How have you experienced Him in your life or surroundings? Write down what is going well for you right now.

_____

_____

_____

_____

_____

_____

_____

_____

Gratitude Game

Stay in Your Lane

In this life we are only in competition with ourselves. Watch Olympic swimmers; they can do nothing about the swimmer next to them. The only thing they can do is stay in their lane, do the best that they can, and focus on their own win. Think about people in your life who you may compare yourself with, and write about how you will take your eyes off of them and put them back on your own journey instead.

_____

_____

_____

_____

_____

_____

_____

_____

_____

_____

_____

_____

_____

_____

_____

_____

_____

_____

_____

Time to Pray

This is a special place of hope, victory, and healing. It is your opportunity to ask the Holy Spirit to move in certain situations or relationships. Rather than filing your complaints, tell Him how you'd like these situations and relationships to look. Jot down four specific requests below, thanking God as if they have already happened.

1 _____

_____

_____

2 _____

_____

_____

3 _____

_____

_____

4 _____

_____

_____

Time to Listen

You asked the Holy Spirit to move. Now listen to God's voice. You can add music or keep it silent. Take a few deep breaths, close your eyes, relax your body, and slow your mind. Make it a goal to sit in silence, breathing deeply, for five to ten minutes each day.

Time to Write

Did you sense God speaking to you? What do you believe He is calling you to do? Do you feel excited? Conflicted? Peaceful? Did anyone come to mind? Did you get a new idea? Now is the time to write it all down!

_____

_____

_____

_____

_____

_____

_____

_____

_____

_____

_____

_____

_____

_____

_____

_____

_____

_____

_____

_____

Dream Life Goal

Writing your goal down each and every day creates momentum over time. Use this space to write down your current Dream Life Goal as you focus on making progress in one area of life at a time.

_____

_____

_____

_____

_____

Say It

Who will you be, how will you feel, and what will your life look like when your goal is complete? Write down the affirmations that correspond to the person you are becoming and the life you are creating. When you're done, read these affirmations out loud to yourself. (Remember to check out the list of affirmations on page 246 for ideas.)

I am _____.

I am _____.

I am _____.

I am _____.

Picture It

Cement your big goal in your mind by picturing yourself achieving it. Take a few deep breaths, and picture what your life will look like when your goal is complete. Notice any new details you can see today.

Do It

Dream Life Goal Action Items

Create a to-do list that is specific to your current goal. Taking action-oriented steps each day will take you one step closer to your goal. Be sure that your actions are small enough to complete in one day, and check them off when they are done!

- [ ] _____
- [ ] _____
- [ ] _____
- [ ] _____
- [ ] _____

Relationship Action Items

What can you do today to be more intentional about important relationships? Thank a teacher, parent, or friend? Do something fun for someone you care about? Show kindness to someone during the day?

- [ ] _____
- [ ] _____

Health Action Items

What actions will you take to improve your physical health? Is it to increase your water intake? Make more time for exercise? Tweak your menu or your sleep time? Log your progress today on the health tracker at the end of the book.

Day
18

It's one of the

greatest gifts

you can give
yourself,

to *forgive.*

Forgive everybody.

Maya Angelou

Prayer

Thank You, God, for Your amazing power and work within my life. Thank You for the love that surrounds me every day. Thank You for being with me and for guiding every decision I make. Please give me the courage to do what is right, remind me of all the people in my life who care, and help me to love myself every day.

Eyes Wide Open

Take a few moments to consider how God has made His presence known in your life lately. What prayers has He answered for you? How have you experienced Him in your life or surroundings? Write down what is going well for you right now.

_____

_____

_____

_____

_____

_____

_____

Gratitude Game

Guilt Be Gone

We all make mistakes. Sometimes we think about a past mistake over and over and over again, but this is neither helpful, productive, nor healthy! Today write a letter to yourself, forgiving yourself for any and all mistakes you may have

made. You did the best that you could with the information that you had, and now that you know better, you will do
better.

Dear Me,

I am sad that _____

_____

_____

_____

_____

_____.

I wish I would have done this instead: _____

_____

_____

_____

_____.

I didn't, but I forgive myself because _____

_____

_____

_____

_____.

I know I did the best that I could with the information I had
at that time. Forgiveness is a daily choice I make for myself,
and now that I have made it, I am free!

Time to Pray

This is a special place of hope, victory, and healing. It is your opportunity to ask the Holy Spirit to move in certain situations or relationships. Rather than filing your complaints, tell Him how you'd like these situations and relationships to look. Jot down four specific requests below, thanking God as if they have already happened.

1
_____

_____

_____

2
_____

_____

_____

3
_____

_____

_____

4
_____

_____

_____

Time to Listen

You asked the Holy Spirit to move. Now listen to God's voice. You can add music or keep it silent. Take a few deep breaths, close your eyes, relax your body, and slow your mind. Make it a goal to sit in silence, breathing deeply, for five to ten minutes each day.

Time to Write

Did you sense God speaking to you? What do you believe He is calling you to do? Do you feel excited? Conflicted? Peaceful? Did anyone come to mind? Did you get a new idea? Now is the time to write it all down!

_____

_____

_____

_____

_____

_____

_____

_____

_____

_____

_____

_____

_____

_____

_____

_____

_____

_____

_____

Dream Life Goal

Writing your goal down each and every day creates momentum over time. Use this space to write down your current Dream Life Goal as you focus on making progress in one area of life at a time.

_____

_____

_____

_____

_____

Say It

Who will you be, how will you feel, and what will your life look like when your goal is complete? Write down the affirmations that correspond to the person you are becoming and the life you are creating. When you're done, read these affirmations out loud to yourself. (Remember to check out the list of affirmations on page 246 for ideas.)

I am _____.

I am _____.

I am _____.

I am _____.

Picture It

Cement your big goal in your mind by picturing yourself achieving it. Take a few deep breaths, and picture what your life will look like when your goal is complete. Notice any new details you can see today.

Do It

Dream Life Goal Action Items

Create a to-do list that is specific to your current goal. Taking action-oriented steps each day will take you one step closer to your goal. Be sure that your actions are small enough to complete in one day, and check them off when they are done!

☐ _____

☐ _____

☐ _____

☐ _____

☐ _____

Relationship Action Items

What can you do today to be more intentional about important relationships? Thank a teacher, parent, or friend? Do something fun for someone you care about? Show kindness to someone during the day?

☐ _____

☐ _____

Health Action Items

What actions will you take to improve your physical health? Is it to increase your water intake? Make more time for exercise? Tweak your menu or your sleep time? Log your progress today on the health tracker at the end of the book.

And now
these three remain:

faith, hope,

and *love.*

but the greatest
of these is

love.

1 Corinthians 13:13

Prayer

Thank You, God, for Your amazing power and work within my life. Thank You for the love that surrounds me every day. Thank You for being with me and for guiding every decision I make. Please give me the courage to do what is right, remind me of all the people in my life who care, and help me to love myself every day.

Eyes Wide Open

Take a few moments to consider how God has made His presence known in your life lately. What prayers has He answered for you? How have you experienced Him in your life or surroundings? Write down what is going well for you right now.

_____

_____

_____

_____

_____

_____

_____

_____

Gratitude Game

The Power of Music

Name a few songs that lift you up immediately when you hear them. Why do you love them so much? Do you play them often? Write about how you feel when you listen to those songs. Play and sing them loudly today and pay attention to how they make you feel.

Time to Pray

This is a special place of hope, victory, and healing. It is your opportunity to ask the Holy Spirit to move in certain situations or relationships. Rather than filing your complaints, tell Him how you'd like these situations and relationships to look. Jot down four specific requests below, thanking God as if they have already happened.

1 _____
_____
_____

2 _____
_____
_____

3 _____
_____
_____

4 _____
_____
_____

Time to Listen

You asked the Holy Spirit to move. Now listen to God's voice. You can add music or keep it silent. Take a few deep breaths, close your eyes, relax your body, and slow your mind. Make it a goal to sit in silence, breathing deeply, for five to ten minutes each day.

Time to Write

Did you sense God speaking to you? What do you believe He is calling you to do? Do you feel excited? Conflicted? Peaceful? Did anyone come to mind? Did you get a new idea? Now is the time to write it all down!

_____

_____

_____

_____

_____

_____

_____

_____

_____

_____

_____

_____

_____

_____

_____

_____

_____

_____

_____

Dream Life Goal

Writing your goal down each and every day creates momentum over time. Use this space to write down your current Dream Life Goal as you focus on making progress in one area of life at a time.

_____

_____

_____

_____

_____

Say It

Who will you be, how will you feel, and what will your life look like when your goal is complete? Write down the affirmations that correspond to the person you are becoming and the life you are creating. When you're done, read these affirmations out loud to yourself. (Remember to check out the list of affirmations on page 246 for ideas.)

I am _____,

I am _____,

I am _____,

I am _____,

Picture It

Cement your big goal in your mind by picturing yourself achieving it. Take a few deep breaths, and picture what your life will look like when your goal is complete. Notice any new details you can see today.

Do It

Dream Life Goal Action Items

Create a to-do list that is specific to your current goal. Taking action-oriented steps each day will take you one step closer to your goal. Be sure that your actions are small enough to complete in one day, and check them off when they are done!

- [ ] _____
- [ ] _____
- [ ] _____
- [ ] _____
- [ ] _____

Relationship Action Items

What can you do today to be more intentional about important relationships? Thank a teacher, parent, or friend? Do something fun for someone you care about? Show kindness to someone during the day?

- [ ] _____
- [ ] _____

Health Action Items

What actions will you take to improve your physical health? Is it to increase your water intake? Make more time for exercise? Tweak your menu or your sleep time? Log your progress today on the health tracker at the end of the book.

Day
20

Do not conform to the

pattern

of this world, but be

transformed

by the

renewing

of your

mind.

Romans 12:2

Prayer

Thank You, God, for Your amazing power and work within my life. Thank You for the love that surrounds me every day. Thank You for being with me and for guiding every decision I make. Please give me the courage to do what is right, remind me of all the people in my life who care, and help me to love myself every day.

Eyes Wide Open

Take a few moments to consider how God has made His presence known in your life lately. What prayers has He answered for you? How have you experienced Him in your life or surroundings? Write down what is going well for you right now.

_____

_____

_____

_____

_____

_____

_____

_____

Gratitude Game

Speak Life to Others

You can choose to live in the world of dreams instead of the world of drama. Talking about people behind their backs is one way to live in the world of drama. So today, make the decision to live in the world of dreams by choosing to say nice things to others.

Think about the people you will see and interact with today, and write down ways you can compliment them. Then consider how avoiding the world of drama will impact your everyday life and relationships.

As you go about your day, if someone starts to gossip to you about someone else, change the subject.

_____

_____

_____

_____

_____

_____

_____

_____

_____

_____

_____

_____

_____

_____

_____

_____

_____

_____

Time to Pray

This is a special place of hope, victory, and healing. It is your opportunity to ask the Holy Spirit to move in certain situations or relationships. Rather than filing your complaints, tell Him how you'd like these situations and relationships to look. Jot down four specific requests below, thanking God as if they have already happened.

1 _____

_____

_____

2 _____

_____

_____

3 _____

_____

_____

4 _____

_____

_____

Time to Listen

You asked the Holy Spirit to move. Now listen to God's voice. You can add music or keep it silent. Take a few deep breaths, close your eyes, relax your body, and slow your mind. Make it a goal to sit in silence, breathing deeply, for five to ten minutes each day.

Time to Write

Did you sense God speaking to you? What do you believe He is calling you to do? Do you feel excited? Conflicted? Peaceful? Did anyone come to mind? Did you get a new idea? Now is the time to write it all down!

_____

_____

_____

_____

_____

_____

_____

_____

_____

_____

_____

_____

_____

_____

_____

_____

_____

_____

Dream Life Goal

Writing your goal down each and every day creates momentum over time. Use this space to write down your current Dream Life Goal as you focus on making progress in one area of life at a time.

_____

_____

_____

_____

_____

Say It

Who will you be, how will you feel, and what will your life look like when your goal is complete? Write down the affirmations that correspond to the person you are becoming and the life you are creating. When you're done, read these affirmations out loud to yourself. (Remember to check out the list of affirmations on page 246 for ideas.)

I am _____.

I am _____.

I am _____.

I am _____.

Picture It

Cement your big goal in your mind by picturing yourself achieving it. Take a few deep breaths, and picture what your life will look like when your goal is complete. Notice any new details you can see today.

Do It

Dream Life Goal Action Items

Create a to-do list that is specific to your current goal. Taking action-oriented steps each day will take you one step closer to your goal. Be sure that your actions are small enough to complete in one day, and check them off when they are done!

- [ ] _____
- [ ] _____
- [ ] _____
- [ ] _____
- [ ] _____

Relationship Action Items

What can you do today to be more intentional about important relationships? Thank a teacher, parent, or friend? Do something fun for someone you care about? Show kindness to someone during the day?

- [ ] _____
- [ ] _____

Health Action Items

What actions will you take to improve your physical health? Is it to increase your water intake? Make more time for exercise? Tweak your menu or your sleep time? Log your progress today on the health tracker at the end of the book.

The
greatest day
in your life and mine is
when we take
total responsibility
for our *attitudes.*

That's the day we
truly grow up.

John C. Maxwell

Prayer

Thank You, God, for Your amazing power and work within my life. Thank You for the love that surrounds me every day. Thank You for being with me and for guiding every decision I make. Please give me the courage to do what is right, remind me of all the people in my life who care, and help me to love myself every day.

Eyes Wide Open

Take a few moments to consider how God has made His presence known in your life lately. What prayers has He answered for you? How have you experienced Him in your life or surroundings? Write down what is going well for you right now.

_____

_____

_____

_____

_____

_____

_____

Gratitude Game

Never Stuck

Envy is often a sign that someone else is making something a priority, and you are not. Name something that you are envious or jealous of in someone else, and write about how you can do or have more of that in your life too.

Time to Pray

This is a special place of hope, victory, and healing. It is your opportunity to ask the Holy Spirit to move in certain situations or relationships. Rather than filing your complaints, tell Him how you'd like these situations and relationships to look. Jot down four specific requests below, thanking God as if they have already happened.

1 _____

_____

_____

2 _____

_____

_____

3 _____

_____

_____

4 _____

_____

_____

Time to Listen

You asked the Holy Spirit to move. Now listen to God's voice. You can add music or keep it silent. Take a few deep breaths, close your eyes, relax your body, and slow your mind. Make it a goal to sit in silence, breathing deeply, for five to ten minutes each day.

Time to Write

Did you sense God speaking to you? What do you believe He is calling you to do? Do you feel excited? Conflicted? Peaceful? Did anyone come to mind? Did you get a new idea? Now is the time to write it all down!

_____

_____

_____

_____

_____

_____

_____

_____

_____

_____

_____

_____

_____

_____

_____

_____

_____

_____

Dream Life Goal

Writing your goal down each and every day creates momentum over time. Use this space to write down your current Dream Life Goal as you focus on making progress in one area of life at a time.

_____

_____

_____

_____

_____

Say It

Who will you be, how will you feel, and what will your life look like when your goal is complete? Write down the affirmations that correspond to the person you are becoming and the life you are creating. When you're done, read these affirmations out loud to yourself. (Remember to check out the list of affirmations on page 246 for ideas.)

I am _____.

I am _____.

I am _____.

I am _____.

Picture It

Cement your big goal in your mind by picturing yourself achieving it. Take a few deep breaths, and picture what your life will look like when your goal is complete. Notice any new details you can see today.

Do It

Dream Life Goal Action Items

Create a to-do list that is specific to your current goal. Taking action-oriented steps each day will take you one step closer to your goal. Be sure that your actions are small enough to complete in one day, and check them off when they are done!

☐ _____

☐ _____

☐ _____

☐ _____

☐ _____

Relationship Action Items

What can you do today to be more intentional about important relationships? Thank a teacher, parent, or friend? Do something fun for someone you care about? Show kindness to someone during the day?

☐ _____

☐ _____

Health Action Items

What actions will you take to improve your physical health? Is it to increase your water intake? Make more time for exercise? Tweak your menu or your sleep time? Log your progress today on the health tracker at the end of the book.

Day
22

A

best friend

is one who brings
out the

best in me.

Henry Ford

Prayer

Thank You, God, for Your amazing power and work within my life. Thank You for the love that surrounds me every day. Thank You for being with me and for guiding every decision I make. Please give me the courage to do what is right, remind me of all the people in my life who care, and help me to love myself every day.

Eyes Wide Open

Take a few moments to consider how God has made His presence known in your life lately. What prayers has He answered for you? How have you experienced Him in your life or surroundings? Write down what is going well for you right now.

_____

_____

_____

_____

_____

_____

_____

Gratitude Game

Smile Big

Who are three people who make you smile? Write down who they are and why they make you smile. Why are they important to you, and how do they impact your life?

Time to Pray

This is a special place of hope, victory, and healing. It is your opportunity to ask the Holy Spirit to move in certain situations or relationships. Rather than filing your complaints, tell Him how you'd like these situations and relationships to look. Jot down four specific requests below, thanking God as if they have already happened.

1 _____

_____

_____

2 _____

_____

_____

3 _____

_____

_____

4 _____

_____

_____

Time to Listen

You asked the Holy Spirit to move. Now listen to God's voice. You can add music or keep it silent. Take a few deep breaths, close your eyes, relax your body, and slow your mind. Make it a goal to sit in silence, breathing deeply, for five to ten minutes each day.

Time to Write

Did you sense God speaking to you? What do you believe He is calling you to do? Do you feel excited? Conflicted? Peaceful? Did anyone come to mind? Did you get a new idea? Now is the time to write it all down!

_____

_____

_____

_____

_____

_____

_____

_____

_____

_____

_____

_____

_____

_____

_____

_____

_____

_____

_____

Dream Life Goal

Writing your goal down each and every day creates momentum over time. Use this space to write down your current Dream Life Goal as you focus on making progress in one area of life at a time.

_____

_____

_____

_____

_____

Say It

Who will you be, how will you feel, and what will your life look like when your goal is complete? Write down the affirmations that correspond to the person you are becoming and the life you are creating. When you're done, read these affirmations out loud to yourself. (Remember to check out the list of affirmations on page 246 for ideas.)

I am _____,

I am _____,

I am _____,

I am _____,

Picture It

Cement your big goal in your mind by picturing yourself achieving it. Take a few deep breaths, and picture what your life will look like when your goal is complete. Notice any new details you can see today.

Do It

Dream Life Goal Action Items

Create a to-do list that is specific to your current goal. Taking action-oriented steps each day will take you one step closer to your goal. Be sure that your actions are small enough to complete in one day, and check them off when they are done!

- [ ] _____
- [ ] _____
- [ ] _____
- [ ] _____
- [ ] _____

Relationship Action Items

What can you do today to be more intentional about important relationships? Thank a teacher, parent, or friend? Do something fun for someone you care about? Show kindness to someone during the day?

- [ ] _____
- [ ] _____

Health Action Items

What actions will you take to improve your physical health? Is it to increase your water intake? Make more time for exercise? Tweak your menu or your sleep time? Log your progress today on the health tracker at the end of the book.

Good communication
must be

HOT —

honest, open,

and

two-way.

Dan Oswald

Prayer

Thank You, God, for Your amazing power and work within my life. Thank You for the love that surrounds me every day. Thank You for being with me and for guiding every decision I make. Please give me the courage to do what is right, remind me of all the people in my life who care, and help me to love myself every day.

Eyes Wide Open

Take a few moments to consider how God has made His presence known in your life lately. What prayers has He answered for you? How have you experienced Him in your life or surroundings? Write down what is going well for you right now.

_____

_____

_____

_____

_____

_____

_____

_____

Gratitude Game

Friendship 101

What qualities do you value most in a friendship? How do you try to show these qualities in your relationships?

Time to Pray

This is a special place of hope, victory, and healing. It is your opportunity to ask the Holy Spirit to move in certain situations or relationships. Rather than filing your complaints, tell Him how you'd like these situations and relationships to look. Jot down four specific requests below, thanking God as if they have already happened.

1
_____

_____

_____

2
_____

_____

_____

3
_____

_____

_____

4
_____

_____

_____

Time to Listen

You asked the Holy Spirit to move. Now listen to God's voice. You can add music or keep it silent. Take a few deep breaths, close your eyes, relax your body, and slow your mind. Make it a goal to sit in silence, breathing deeply, for five to ten minutes each day.

Time to Write

Did you sense God speaking to you? What do you believe He is calling you to do? Do you feel excited? Conflicted? Peaceful? Did anyone come to mind? Did you get a new idea? Now is the time to write it all down!

_____

_____

_____

_____

_____

_____

_____

_____

_____

_____

_____

_____

_____

_____

_____

_____

_____

_____

Dream Life Goal

Writing your goal down each and every day creates momentum over time. Use this space to write down your current Dream Life Goal as you focus on making progress in one area of life at a time.

_____

_____

_____

_____

_____

Say It

Who will you be, how will you feel, and what will your life look like when your goal is complete? Write down the affirmations that correspond to the person you are becoming and the life you are creating. When you're done, read these affirmations out loud to yourself. (Remember to check out the list of affirmations on page 246 for ideas.)

I am _____.

I am _____.

I am _____.

I am _____.

Picture It

Cement your big goal in your mind by picturing yourself achieving it. Take a few deep breaths, and picture what your life will look like when your goal is complete. Notice any new details you can see today.

Do It

Dream Life Goal Action Items

Create a to-do list that is specific to your current goal. Taking action-oriented steps each day will take you one step closer to your goal. Be sure that your actions are small enough to complete in one day, and check them off when they are done!

- ☐ _____
- ☐ _____
- ☐ _____
- ☐ _____
- ☐ _____

Relationship Action Items

What can you do today to be more intentional about important relationships? Thank a teacher, parent, or friend? Do something fun for someone you care about? Show kindness to someone during the day?

- ☐ _____
- ☐ _____

Health Action Items

What actions will you take to improve your physical health? Is it to increase your water intake? Make more time for exercise? Tweak your menu or your sleep time? Log your progress today on the health tracker at the end of the book.

Death and
life
are in the
power
of the tongue.

Proverbs 18:21, ESV

Prayer

Thank You, God, for Your amazing power and work within my life. Thank You for the love that surrounds me every day. Thank You for being with me and for guiding every decision I make. Please give me the courage to do what is right, remind me of all the people in my life who care, and help me to love myself every day.

Eyes Wide Open

Take a few moments to consider how God has made His presence known in your life lately. What prayers has He answered for you? How have you experienced Him in your life or surroundings? Write down what is going well for you right now.

_____

_____

_____

_____

_____

_____

_____

Gratitude Game

Speak Life to Yourself

The way you speak to yourself matters. Sometimes we say things to ourselves that we would never say to another person. Today write a list of all the things you love about yourself, things you are grateful for in your life, and what you are most excited about. Try to list at least fifty things.

Time to Pray

This is a special place of hope, victory, and healing. It is your opportunity to ask the Holy Spirit to move in certain situations or relationships. Rather than filing your complaints, tell Him how you'd like these situations and relationships to look. Jot down four specific requests below, thanking God as if they have already happened.

1 _____

_____

_____

2 _____

_____

_____

3 _____

_____

_____

4 _____

_____

_____

Time to Listen

You asked the Holy Spirit to move. Now listen to God's voice. You can add music or keep it silent. Take a few deep breaths, close your eyes, relax your body, and slow your mind. Make it a goal to sit in silence, breathing deeply, for five to ten minutes each day.

Time to Write

Did you sense God speaking to you? What do you believe He is calling you to do? Do you feel excited? Conflicted? Peaceful? Did anyone come to mind? Did you get a new idea? Now is the time to write it all down!

_____

_____

_____

_____

_____

_____

_____

_____

_____

_____

_____

_____

_____

_____

_____

_____

_____

_____

_____

Dream Life Goal

Writing your goal down each and every day creates momentum over time. Use this space to write down your current Dream Life Goal as you focus on making progress in one area of life at a time.

_____

_____

_____

_____

_____

Say It

Who will you be, how will you feel, and what will your life look like when your goal is complete? Write down the affirmations that correspond to the person you are becoming and the life you are creating. When you're done, read these affirmations out loud to yourself. (Remember to check out the list of affirmations on page 246 for ideas.)

I am _____.

I am _____.

I am _____.

I am _____.

Picture It

Cement your big goal in your mind by picturing yourself achieving it. Take a few deep breaths, and picture what your life will look like when your goal is complete. Notice any new details you can see today.

Do It

Dream Life Goal Action Items

Create a to-do list that is specific to your current goal. Taking action-oriented steps each day will take you one step closer to your goal. Be sure that your actions are small enough to complete in one day, and check them off when they are done!

- [ ] _____
- [ ] _____
- [ ] _____
- [ ] _____
- [ ] _____

Relationship Action Items

What can you do today to be more intentional about important relationships? Thank a teacher, parent, or friend? Do something fun for someone you care about? Show kindness to someone during the day?

- [ ] _____
- [ ] _____

Health Action Items

What actions will you take to improve your physical health? Is it to increase your water intake? Make more time for exercise? Tweak your menu or your sleep time? Log your progress today on the health tracker at the end of the book.

Feel
the fear, and
do it
anyway.

Susan Jeffers

Prayer

Thank You, God, for Your amazing power and work within my life. Thank You for the love that surrounds me every day. Thank You for being with me and for guiding every decision I make. Please give me the courage to do what is right, remind me of all the people in my life who care, and help me to love myself every day.

Eyes Wide Open

Take a few moments to consider how God has made His presence known in your life lately. What prayers has He answered for you? How have you experienced Him in your life or surroundings? Write down what is going well for you right now.

_____

_____

_____

_____

_____

_____

_____

Gratitude Game

Letting Go

It is understandable to be upset when someone has wronged you, but holding on to the anger hurts only you in the long run. Today write a letter to someone who has hurt your feelings. Let that person know how he or she hurt you, and tell him or her that you do not want him or her to do it again. Finish by telling the person that you forgive him or her. Once you're finished, you can rip up the letter and throw it away.

If this stirs up some strong emotions and you find you need extra support, please reach out to a trusted adult or counselor.

Dear _____.

I am angry and hurt that _____

_____

_____

_____

_____

_____

_____

_____.

I wish you would have _____

_____

_____

_____

_____

_____

_____,

but you didn't. I choose to forgive you. Now that I have made that choice, I am free!

Time to Pray

This is a special place of hope, victory, and healing. It is your opportunity to ask the Holy Spirit to move in certain situations or relationships. Rather than filing your complaints, tell Him how you'd like these situations and relationships to look. Jot down four specific requests below, thanking God as if they have already happened.

1 _____

_____

_____

2 _____

_____

_____

3 _____

_____

_____

4 _____

_____

_____

Time to Listen

You asked the Holy Spirit to move. Now listen to God's voice. You can add music or keep it silent. Take a few deep breaths, close your eyes, relax your body, and slow your mind. Make it a goal to sit in silence, breathing deeply, for five to ten minutes each day.

Time to Write

Did you sense God speaking to you? What do you believe He is calling you to do? Do you feel excited? Conflicted? Peaceful? Did anyone come to mind? Did you get a new idea? Now is the time to write it all down!

_____

_____

_____

_____

_____

_____

_____

_____

_____

_____

_____

_____

_____

_____

_____

_____

_____

_____

Dream Life Goal

Writing your goal down each and every day creates momentum over time. Use this space to write down your current Dream Life Goal as you focus on making progress in one area of life at a time.

_____

_____

_____

_____

_____

Say It

Who will you be, how will you feel, and what will your life look like when your goal is complete? Write down the affirmations that correspond to the person you are becoming and the life you are creating. When you're done, read these affirmations out loud to yourself. (Remember to check out the list of affirmations on page 246 for ideas.)

I am _____.

I am _____.

I am _____.

I am _____.

Picture It

Cement your big goal in your mind by picturing yourself achieving it. Take a few deep breaths, and picture what your life will look like when your goal is complete. Notice any new details you can see today.

Do It

Dream Life Goal Action Items

Create a to-do list that is specific to your current goal. Taking action-oriented steps each day will take you one step closer to your goal. Be sure that your actions are small enough to complete in one day, and check them off when they are done!

- [ ] _____
- [ ] _____
- [ ] _____
- [ ] _____
- [ ] _____

Relationship Action Items

What can you do today to be more intentional about important relationships? Thank a teacher, parent, or friend? Do something fun for someone you care about? Show kindness to someone during the day?

- [ ] _____
- [ ] _____

Health Action Items

What actions will you take to improve your physical health? Is it to increase your water intake? Make more time for exercise? Tweak your menu or your sleep time? Log your progress today on the health tracker at the end of the book.

Day 26

Do whatever *you can,* with what *you have,* where *you are.*

Bill Widener

Prayer

Thank You, God, for Your amazing power and work within my life. Thank You for the love that surrounds me every day. Thank You for being with me and for guiding every decision I make. Please give me the courage to do what is right, remind me of all the people in my life who care, and help me to love myself every day.

Eyes Wide Open

Take a few moments to consider how God has made His presence known in your life lately. What prayers has He answered for you? How have you experienced Him in your life or surroundings? Write down what is going well for you right now.

_____

_____

_____

_____

_____

_____

_____

_____

Gratitude Game

Write Your Obituary

When you die, what do you want to be remembered for? What legacy do you want to leave behind with your attitude, actions, and relationships? Consider these questions and then write an imaginary obituary for yourself.

Time to Pray

This is a special place of hope, victory, and healing. It is your opportunity to ask the Holy Spirit to move in certain situations or relationships. Rather than filing your complaints, tell Him how you'd like these situations and relationships to look. Jot down four specific requests below, thanking God as if they have already happened.

1 _____

_____

_____

2 _____

_____

_____

3 _____

_____

_____

4 _____

_____

_____

Time to Listen

You asked the Holy Spirit to move. Now listen to God's voice. You can add music or keep it silent. Take a few deep breaths, close your eyes, relax your body, and slow your mind. Make it a goal to sit in silence, breathing deeply, for five to ten minutes each day.

Time to Write

Did you sense God speaking to you? What do you believe He is calling you to do? Do you feel excited? Conflicted? Peaceful? Did anyone come to mind? Did you get a new idea? Now is the time to write it all down!

_____

_____

_____

_____

_____

_____

_____

_____

_____

_____

_____

_____

_____

_____

_____

_____

_____

_____

Dream Life Goal

Writing your goal down each and every day creates momentum over time. Use this space to write down your current Dream Life Goal as you focus on making progress in one area of life at a time.

_____

_____

_____

_____

_____

Say It

Who will you be, how will you feel, and what will your life look like when your goal is complete? Write down the affirmations that correspond to the person you are becoming and the life you are creating. When you're done, read these affirmations out loud to yourself. (Remember to check out the list of affirmations on page 246 for ideas.)

I am _____.

I am _____.

I am _____.

I am _____.

Picture It

Cement your big goal in your mind by picturing yourself achieving it. Take a few deep breaths, and picture what your life will look like when your goal is complete. Notice any new details you can see today.

Do It

Dream Life Goal Action Items

Create a to-do list that is specific to your current goal. Taking action-oriented steps each day will take you one step closer to your goal. Be sure that your actions are small enough to complete in one day, and check them off when they are done!

- ☐ _____
- ☐ _____
- ☐ _____
- ☐ _____
- ☐ _____

Relationship Action Items

What can you do today to be more intentional about important relationships? Thank a teacher, parent, or friend? Do something fun for someone you care about? Show kindness to someone during the day?

- ☐ _____
- ☐ _____

Health Action Items

What actions will you take to improve your physical health? Is it to increase your water intake? Make more time for exercise? Tweak your menu or your sleep time? Log your progress today on the health tracker at the end of the book.

Day 27

Ask

and it will be
given to you;

seek

and you will find;

knock

and the door will
be opened to you.

Matthew 7:7

Prayer

Thank You, God, for Your amazing power and work within my life. Thank You for the love that surrounds me every day. Thank You for being with me and for guiding every decision I make. Please give me the courage to do what is right, remind me of all the people in my life who care, and help me to love myself every day.

Eyes Wide Open

Take a few moments to consider how God has made His presence known in your life lately. What prayers has He answered for you? How have you experienced Him in your life or surroundings? Write down what is going well for you right now.

_____

_____

_____

_____

_____

_____

_____

_____

Gratitude Game

Interesting Person

Who is someone you look up to? What qualities and characteristics make this person interesting to you? How can you learn even more from them?

Time to Pray

This is a special place of hope, victory, and healing. It is your opportunity to ask the Holy Spirit to move in certain situations or relationships. Rather than filing your complaints, tell Him how you'd like these situations and relationships to look. Jot down four specific requests below, thanking God as if they have already happened.

1 _____

_____

_____

2 _____

_____

_____

3 _____

_____

_____

4 _____

_____

_____

Time to Listen

You asked the Holy Spirit to move. Now listen to God's voice. You can add music or keep it silent. Take a few deep breaths, close your eyes, relax your body, and slow your mind. Make it a goal to sit in silence, breathing deeply, for five to ten minutes each day.

Time to Write

Did you sense God speaking to you? What do you believe He is calling you to do? Do you feel excited? Conflicted? Peaceful? Did anyone come to mind? Did you get a new idea? Now is the time to write it all down!

Dream Life Goal

Writing your goal down each and every day creates momentum over time. Use this space to write down your current Dream Life Goal as you focus on making progress in one area of life at a time.

_____

_____

_____

_____

_____

Say It

Who will you be, how will you feel, and what will your life look like when your goal is complete? Write down the affirmations that correspond to the person you are becoming and the life you are creating. When you're done, read these affirmations out loud to yourself. (Remember to check out the list of affirmations on page 246 for ideas.)

I am _____.

I am _____.

I am _____.

I am _____.

Picture It

Cement your big goal in your mind by picturing yourself achieving it. Take a few deep breaths, and picture what your life will look like when your goal is complete. Notice any new details you can see today.

Do It

Dream Life Goal Action Items

Create a to-do list that is specific to your current goal. Taking action-oriented steps each day will take you one step closer to your goal. Be sure that your actions are small enough to complete in one day, and check them off when they are done!

- [ ] _____
- [ ] _____
- [ ] _____
- [ ] _____
- [ ] _____

Relationship Action Items

What can you do today to be more intentional about important relationships? Thank a teacher, parent, or friend? Do something fun for someone you care about? Show kindness to someone during the day?

- [ ] _____
- [ ] _____

Health Action Items

What actions will you take to improve your physical health? Is it to increase your water intake? Make more time for exercise? Tweak your menu or your sleep time? Log your progress today on the health tracker at the end of the book.

Be true to your

word

and your

work

and your

friend.

John Boyle O'Reilly

Prayer

Thank You, God, for Your amazing power and work within my life. Thank You for the love that surrounds me every day. Thank You for being with me and for guiding every decision I make. Please give me the courage to do what is right, remind me of all the people in my life who care, and help me to love myself every day.

Eyes Wide Open

Take a few moments to consider how God has made His presence known in your life lately. What prayers has He answered for you? How have you experienced Him in your life or surroundings? Write down what is going well for you right now.

_____

_____

_____

_____

_____

_____

_____

Gratitude Game

Best-Case Scenario

Think about the circumstances, relationships, and situations in your life that are hanging in the balance. Instead of thinking about the worst-case scenarios in each case, think about the best-case scenarios. If everything went the best way possible, what would you experience? I recommend writing these results in the present tense, as if things are unfolding perfectly right now.

_____

_____

_____

_____

_____

_____

_____

_____

_____

_____

_____

_____

_____

_____

_____

_____

_____

_____

_____

Time to Pray

This is a special place of hope, victory, and healing. It is your opportunity to ask the Holy Spirit to move in certain situations or relationships. Rather than filing your complaints, tell Him how you'd like these situations and relationships to look. Jot down four specific requests below, thanking God as if they have already happened.

1 _____

_____

_____

2 _____

_____

_____

3 _____

_____

_____

4 _____

_____

_____

Time to Listen

You asked the Holy Spirit to move. Now listen to God's voice. You can add music or keep it silent. Take a few deep breaths, close your eyes, relax your body, and slow your mind. Make it a goal to sit in silence, breathing deeply, for five to ten minutes each day.

Time to Write

Did you sense God speaking to you? What do you believe He is calling you to do? Do you feel excited? Conflicted? Peaceful? Did anyone come to mind? Did you get a new idea? Now is the time to write it all down!

_____

_____

_____

_____

_____

_____

_____

_____

_____

_____

_____

_____

_____

_____

_____

_____

_____

_____

Dream Life Goal

Writing your goal down each and every day creates momentum over time. Use this space to write down your current Dream Life Goal as you focus on making progress in one area of life at a time.

_____

_____

_____

_____

_____

Say It

Who will you be, how will you feel, and what will your life look like when your goal is complete? Write down the affirmations that correspond to the person you are becoming and the life you are creating. When you're done, read these affirmations out loud to yourself. (Remember to check out the list of affirmations on page 246 for ideas.)

I am _____.

I am _____.

I am _____.

I am _____.

Picture It

Cement your big goal in your mind by picturing yourself achieving it. Take a few deep breaths, and picture what your life will look like when your goal is complete. Notice any new details you can see today.

Do It

Dream Life Goal Action Items

Create a to-do list that is specific to your current goal. Taking action-oriented steps each day will take you one step closer to your goal. Be sure that your actions are small enough to complete in one day, and check them off when they are done!

☐ _____

☐ _____

☐ _____

☐ _____

☐ _____

Relationship Action Items

What can you do today to be more intentional about important relationships? Thank a teacher, parent, or friend? Do something fun for someone you care about? Show kindness to someone during the day?

☐ _____

☐ _____

Health Action Items

What actions will you take to improve your physical health? Is it to increase your water intake? Make more time for exercise? Tweak your menu or your sleep time? Log your progress today on the health tracker at the end of the book.

Success

is the sum of

small efforts

repeated

day in

and

day out.

Robert Collier

Prayer

Thank You, God, for Your amazing power and work within my life. Thank You for the love that surrounds me every day. Thank You for being with me and for guiding every decision I make. Please give me the courage to do what is right, remind me of all the people in my life who care, and help me to love myself every day.

Eyes Wide Open

Take a few moments to consider how God has made His presence known in your life lately. What prayers has He answered for you? How have you experienced Him in your life or surroundings? Write down what is going well for you right now.

_____

_____

_____

_____

_____

_____

_____

_____

Gratitude Game

Do I Have Blue Hair?

We tend to take things personally when we are already feeling insecure about a situation. For example, would you get upset if someone said you had blue hair? Probably not, because you know it's not true. You would simply say, "That isn't true." But if someone comments about something you feel unsure about—the way you look, how you dress, or your family, for example—you may react. Think about a time when you took something personally, and write about how you can build confidence in that area of your life.

The situation that I got upset about:

_____

_____

_____

_____

Why did I get upset?

_____

_____

_____

What insecurity did this stir up?

_____

_____

_____

_____

How can I build more confidence in this area?

_____

_____

_____

_____

Time to Pray

This is a special place of hope, victory, and healing. It is your opportunity to ask the Holy Spirit to move in certain situations or relationships. Rather than filing your complaints, tell Him how you'd like these situations and relationships to look. Jot down four specific requests below, thanking God as if they have already happened.

1 _____

_____

_____

2 _____

_____

_____

3 _____

_____

_____

4 _____

_____

_____

Time to Listen

You asked the Holy Spirit to move. Now listen to God's voice. You can add music or keep it silent. Take a few deep breaths, close your eyes, relax your body, and slow your mind. Make it a goal to sit in silence, breathing deeply, for five to ten minutes each day.

Time to Write

Did you sense God speaking to you? What do you believe He is calling you to do? Do you feel excited? Conflicted? Peaceful? Did anyone come to mind? Did you get a new idea? Now is the time to write it all down!

_____

_____

_____

_____

_____

_____

_____

_____

_____

_____

_____

_____

_____

_____

_____

_____

_____

_____

Dream Life Goal

Writing your goal down each and every day creates momentum over time. Use this space to write down your current Dream Life Goal as you focus on making progress in one area of life at a time.

_____

_____

_____

_____

_____

Say It

Who will you be, how will you feel, and what will your life look like when your goal is complete? Write down the affirmations that correspond to the person you are becoming and the life you are creating. When you're done, read these affirmations out loud to yourself. (Remember to check out the list of affirmations on page 246 for ideas.)

I am _____.

I am _____.

I am _____.

I am _____.

Picture It

Cement your big goal in your mind by picturing yourself achieving it. Take a few deep breaths, and picture what your life will look like when your goal is complete. Notice any new details you can see today.

Do It

Dream Life Goal Action Items

Create a to-do list that is specific to your current goal. Taking action-oriented steps each day will take you one step closer to your goal. Be sure that your actions are small enough to complete in one day, and check them off when they are done!

☐ _____

☐ _____

☐ _____

☐ _____

☐ _____

Relationship Action Items

What can you do today to be more intentional about important relationships? Thank a teacher, parent, or friend? Do something fun for someone you care about? Show kindness to someone during the day?

☐ _____

☐ _____

Health Action Items

What actions will you take to improve your physical health? Is it to increase your water intake? Make more time for exercise? Tweak your menu or your sleep time? Log your progress today on the health tracker at the end of the book.

Trust
in the
LORD
with all your
heart.

Proverbs 3:5

Prayer

Thank You, God, for Your amazing power and work within my life. Thank You for the love that surrounds me every day. Thank You for being with me and for guiding every decision I make. Please give me the courage to do what is right, remind me of all the people in my life who care, and help me to love myself every day.

Eyes Wide Open

Take a few moments to consider how God has made His presence known in your life lately. What prayers has He answered for you? How have you experienced Him in your life or surroundings? Write down what is going well for you right now.

_____

_____

_____

_____

_____

_____

_____

Gratitude Game

Future Present

Imagine it is five years from now, and you are writing a letter to yourself. Date the letter five years in the future, and in it describe all the amazing adventures you have experienced in those five years. Be as detailed and emotionally connected to your story as possible.

When you're done, read your letter as often as you can. How do you feel when you read it back to yourself?

_____

_____

_____

_____

_____

_____

_____

_____

_____

_____

_____

_____

_____

_____

_____

_____

_____

_____

Time to Pray

This is a special place of hope, victory, and healing. It is your opportunity to ask the Holy Spirit to move in certain situations or relationships. Rather than filing your complaints, tell Him how you'd like these situations and relationships to look. Jot down four specific requests below, thanking God as if they have already happened.

1 _____

_____

_____

2 _____

_____

_____

3 _____

_____

_____

4 _____

_____

_____

Time to Listen

You asked the Holy Spirit to move. Now listen to God's voice. You can add music or keep it silent. Take a few deep breaths, close your eyes, relax your body, and slow your mind. Make it a goal to sit in silence, breathing deeply, for five to ten minutes each day.

Time to Write

Did you sense God speaking to you? What do you believe He is calling you to do? Do you feel excited? Conflicted? Peaceful? Did anyone come to mind? Did you get a new idea? Now is the time to write it all down!

Dream Life Goal

Writing your goal down each and every day creates momentum over time. Use this space to write down your current Dream Life Goal as you focus on making progress in one area of life at a time.

_____

_____

_____

_____

_____

Say It

Who will you be, how will you feel, and what will your life look like when your goal is complete? Write down the affirmations that correspond to the person you are becoming and the life you are creating. When you're done, read these affirmations out loud to yourself. (Remember to check out the list of affirmations on page 246 for ideas.)

I am _____.

I am _____.

I am _____.

I am _____.

Picture It

Cement your big goal in your mind by picturing yourself achieving it. Take a few deep breaths, and picture what your life will look like when your goal is complete. Notice any new details you can see today.

Do It

Dream Life Goal Action Items

Create a to-do list that is specific to your current goal. Taking action-oriented steps each day will take you one step closer to your goal. Be sure that your actions are small enough to complete in one day, and check them off when they are done!

- ☐ _____
- ☐ _____
- ☐ _____
- ☐ _____
- ☐ _____

Relationship Action Items

What can you do today to be more intentional about important relationships? Thank a teacher, parent, or friend? Do something fun for someone you care about? Show kindness to someone during the day?

- ☐ _____
- ☐ _____

Health Action Items

What actions will you take to improve your physical health? Is it to increase your water intake? Make more time for exercise? Tweak your menu or your sleep time? Log your progress today on the health tracker at the end of the book.

Conclusion

Congratulations! You are thirty days closer to living your dream life!

During the last month we have spent together, you have made and cemented habits that will change your life forever. Keep this going. These new habits are sending you down a new path—a path that leads toward success. Don't stop now. Continue connecting with your dream life goal daily and taking time each morning to determine a plan of action and execute it. Pick up another one of the journals in the Dream Life series and go through it, or do this one again. Remember, what the mind sees, the body follows, and consistency will create and rapidly build momentum.

I am so excited you have chosen to allow me to make this journey with you. If you want continued support on your journey, follow me on YouTube or subscribe to my podcast, *Dream Cast*. You can also visit DeniseWalsh.com for additional resources to help you on your way.

Now keep up the momentum, and continue to dream big!

Habit Trackers

Habit trackers are a great way of becoming more mindful about the success habits you are cultivating. Start by circling the month during which you will be logging your activity, and then decide which habits you will focus on: your daily practice goals, water intake, affirmations, time with friends or family, etc. When you complete that task/habit, cross through or color in the box that corresponds to the date.

I have found it's best to focus on one to three new habits at a time. Once they become easier and more automatic, you can add more.

Here's an example. Let's say I want to track my daily prac-tice goal, exercise, sleep, and when I do my affirmations. I would start by writing the habit in the space to the left and then log my progress by shading the numbered boxes. If on the first of the month I got eight hours of sleep, I would color in the box marked 1. In the example below, you can see that I reached my sleep goal on May 1, 3–8, and 10–16 but not on May 2 and 9. Make sense?

Habit	*Month*	Jan	Feb	Mar	Apr	May	June	July
eight hours of sleep		1	2	3	4	5	6	7	8
		9	10	11	12	13	14	15	16

At the end of the month, you'll be able to see how consis-tent you were at prioritizing those practices. Don't forget to celebrate your wins and progress toward new habits!

Habit

Month

Jan | Feb | Mar | Apr | May | Jun | Jul | Aug | Sep | Oct | Nov | Dec

Habit	1	2	3	4	5	6	7	8	9	10	11	12	13	14	15	16
	17	18	19	20	21	22	23	24	25	26	27	28	29	30	31	❤
	1	2	3	4	5	6	7	8	9	10	11	12	13	14	15	16
	17	18	19	20	21	22	23	24	25	26	27	28	29	30	31	❤
	1	2	3	4	5	6	7	8	9	10	11	12	13	14	15	16
	17	18	19	20	21	22	23	24	25	26	27	28	29	30	31	❤
	1	2	3	4	5	6	7	8	9	10	11	12	13	14	15	16
	17	18	19	20	21	22	23	24	25	26	27	28	29	30	31	❤
	1	2	3	4	5	6	7	8	9	10	11	12	13	14	15	16
	17	18	19	20	21	22	23	24	25	26	27	28	29	30	31	❤

Habit

Month	Jan	Feb	Mar	Apr	May	Jun	Jul	Aug	Sep	Oct	Nov	Dec
	1	2	3	4	5	6	7	8	9	10	11	12	13	14	15	16
	17	18	19	20	21	22	23	24	25	26	27	28	29	30	31	❥
	1	2	3	4	5	6	7	8	9	10	11	12	13	14	15	16
	17	18	19	20	21	22	23	24	25	26	27	28	29	30	31	❥
	1	2	3	4	5	6	7	8	9	10	11	12	13	14	15	16
	17	18	19	20	21	22	23	24	25	26	27	28	29	30	31	❥
	1	2	3	4	5	6	7	8	9	10	11	12	13	14	15	16
	17	18	19	20	21	22	23	24	25	26	27	28	29	30	31	❥
	1	2	3	4	5	6	7	8	9	10	11	12	13	14	15	16
	17	18	19	20	21	22	23	24	25	26	27	28	29	30	31	❥

Affirmations

When affirmations are new to us, it can be hard to write them from scratch, so I have compiled a list of my favorites to help you get started and put them on the next page. Notice that they almost always start with "I" or "my." That's because they address how you think about yourself, your dreams, and your goals.

In addition to writing your affirmations in this journal each day, I recommend you cut out the affirmation cards on the pages that follow. Each of them is printed on one side with one of the affirmations in the previous list. The other side is lined so that you can write out your own once you become more comfortable with this practice.

I like to choose three or four at a time and post them in places where I will see them during the day. Your room, car, locker, or notebooks could be great spots. Whenever you see them or think of them, take a moment to recite these affirmations. Out loud is best, but repeating them in your mind is also incredibly powerful. After a month, choose another three or four.

The more consistent you are with this habit, the faster your dream life—and dream self—will become a reality!

I love who I am, and I love who I am becoming.

I am becoming better with each day.

I am happy to be here.

I will ask for help when I need it.

The more I like myself, the more others will like me.

I give myself permission to do what is best for me.

If a situation won't matter in five years, then it doesn't matter today.

I am happy and full of joy.

I love and respect my family for everything that they do and have done for me.

I am responsible with my technology.

My thoughts and opinions matter.

I am proud of myself for doing the hard thing.

My dreams are achievable.

I am enough.

I am lovable.

I have a lot of gifts to offer the world.

I have everything I need to be successful.

This too shall pass.

Everything works out for the best possible good.

I can do whatever I focus my mind on.

Today is the best day of my life.

I choose to spend time doing things that support myself and others.

I look for ways to add value to others.

I trust myself.

I trust that I will follow through on what I do or say.

I speak life instead of gossip.

I easily and effortlessly excel at school.

I love who I am, and I love who I am becoming.

I am becoming better with each day.

I am happy to be here.

Dream Life Teen Journal

I will ask for help when I need it.

DeniseWalsh.com

✂

Dream Life Teen Journal

I give myself permission to do what is best for me.

DeniseWalsh.com

✂

Dream Life Teen Journal

If a situation won't matter in five years, then it doesn't matter today.

DeniseWalsh.com

I love and respect my family for everything that they do and have done for me.

I am responsible with my technology.

My thoughts and opinions matter.

_____

_____

_____

_____

_____

_____

_____

_____

_____

_____

_____

_____

_____

_____

_____

_____

_____

_____

I am proud of myself for doing the hard thing.

My dreams are achievable.

I am enough.

Dream Life Teen Journal

I am lovable.

Dream Life Teen Journal

I have a lot of gifts to offer the world.

Dream Life Teen Journal

I have everything I need to be successful.

This too shall pass.

Everything works out for the best possible good.

I can do whatever I focus my mind on.

Today is the best day of my life.

I look for ways to add value to others.

I am happy and full of joy.

CPSIA information can be obtained
at www.ICGtesting.com
Printed in the USA
LVHW021536030920
665031LV00013B/952